Chrono Trigger

Chrono Trigger
Michael P. Williams

Boss Fight Books
Los Angeles, CA
bossfightbooks.com

ISBN 13: 978-1-940535-01-2
First Printing: 2014
Second Printing: 2016
Third Printing: 2019

Series Editor: Gabe Durham
Book Design by Ken Baumann
Page Design by Adam Robinson

TABLE OF CONTENTS

FOREWORD

I'M GOING TO MAKE THIS short so you can move along and enjoy what you came here for! The work you will be reading is at once an autobiography, an enthusiast's ode to the early years of gaming, and a coming of age story of boy-meets-cartridge.

This narrative is remarkable to me, not because I figure much into it, but because of how deeply connected the author is with a game I happened to localize while I worked for Squaresoft in the 90s. I was lucky to have been able to "hook my wagon" to the smart and creative teams at Square for a time. Like Michael P. Williams, I look back fondly on those 16-bit works of art, and am glad to have played a small role in making them available outside of Japan.

The art of translation can be characterized as an exercise in channeling, sitting inactive for hours, trying to balance concision, resourcefulness, and faithfulness to the original game. There is always the deadline, as well—that ever-present elephant in the translator's brainpan.

Chrono Trigger was a whopper to translate due to the options available to the player, and how different combinations of characters were designed to interact in different ways. Keeping these interactions in mind along with tone, jokes, and ongoing plot lines was tough, and certainly I made a number of interesting errors along the way.

But I knew while translating that this title was something quite special, that the story and graphics represented an evolution in gaming. I kept having to push back my return to the States due to the game's ongoing localization requirements, but knew the effort would be worth it. The development team at Square had put so much heart and soul into *Chrono Trigger*, it was the least I could to try to do their beautiful game justice.

The cartridge's memory footprint was so big that it was one of the most expensive games ever to ship on the Super NES. A retail price of 80 dollars was a serious investment for gamers, I suppose, but clearly—as seen in the accounts of Williams and countless other *Chrono Trigger* fans in the last nineteen years—the experience was worth the price of admission. And so... on with the story!

Ted Woolsey
Winter, 2014

A NOTE ON THE TEXT

IN GENERAL, THIS VOLUME USES as its basis the first English edition of *Chrono Trigger* translated by Ted Woolsey for the Super Nintendo in 1995. This same text has been used for later editions, such as the North American PlayStation port (released in a bundle as *Final Fantasy Chronicles*) in 2001. For comparison, I have included occasional references to the original Japanese Super Famicom text and to later English editions, including the retranslation prepared by Tom Slattery for the Nintendo DS in 2008. Later ports to various gaming platforms, including the Wii Virtual Console or iOS, have used either of these translations, sometimes with minor alterations to account for new controller interfaces. A quick way to determine which of these English translations you have is to refer to the opening line spoken by Crono's mother. The Woolsey version begins with "Crono… Crono! Good morning, Crono!" The Slattery version starts with "Crono… Crono! Crono, are you still sleeping?"

FORWARD TO THE PAST

AN HOURGLASS MEASURES THE SECONDS on the screen of a newly purchased big-screen television. The music crescendos. An adventure is about to begin.

My sister and mother are downstairs just beginning a hot summer afternoon's episode of *Days of Our Lives*. Me, I've decided to forsake the people of Salem for a different kind of saga. No, today will not be full of surprise brain tumors, satanic possessions, and the insatiable desires of the flesh. Today is not a day for small-time drama. Today is an epic day.

A pendulum measures the seconds on the screen of an old rabbit-eared TV upstairs in my bedroom. The music swells. I press start.

•

I began *Chrono Trigger* the same way I began almost every role-playing game I eventually fell in love with—by reading about it. North American players had to endure agonizing months of anticipation, lapping up whatever blurbs *Nintendo Power* or *Game Informer* dished out until that long-awaited Tuesday, August 22, 1995.

By the time I finally got my hands on *Chrono Trigger* in late 1995, it had already been a year since my last Square fix with the operatic *Final Fantasy III* (really a disguised *FF6*). Don't get me wrong, I devoured *EarthBound*, which had arrived stateside on June 5th that same summer. It was my thirteenth birthday present, in fact. I reveled in its fractured Americana. I laughed out loud at its zany humor. I scratched and sniffed the vile-smelling cards that came in the guidebook.

But to me, Square was the undisputed king of RPGs. Square opened the nexus of worlds—drama, fantasy, cinema, game. Square summoned the power of totems—sword, crystal, airship, chocobo! These hieroglyphs became the language of my inner fantasy stories, the legends of me I told myself in dreams.

Everything I had read about *Chrono Trigger* hyped it up to be the pinnacle of all my RPG desires. The sprawling world design of *Secret of Mana*, the raw emotional storytelling of *Final Fantasy*, the inescapably appealing art design of *Dragon Warrior* (really just the repackaged *Dragon Quest*). *Chrono Trigger* promised to be the epitome of everything I loved about RPGs.

I can't remember if I bought *Chrono Trigger* with my own money or if my mom went out and bought me the game for Christmas. Probably the latter. But when I finally broke the seal on that box, popped the cart into my SNES, and slid that purple power switch on, I knew that *Chrono Trigger* had to be among the most beautiful games that had ever been produced. Armed with my official strategy guide, I was an eager *Chrono*-naut for weeks, pausing only to use the bathroom or to grab a snack. Or to finally figure out just what the hell my mom had been yelling to me from downstairs.

•

"Good morning, Crono!"

A cheerful, banal greeting from a bland, nameless mom. Teenager Crono lives a life of relative peace, if not boredom, with his anonymous mother. But the day into which he awakens, the day we meet him, is the special day he's been waiting for. In fact, he's so excited that he slept in his clothes! Today is the first day of the Millennial Fair. Crono's got money in his pocket and he's ready to make things happen.

Well designed role-playing games are replete with missions to be ignored or embraced. Before his date with destiny and a mysterious girl at the fair—conveniently located right by his home—Crono can see the world around him. He can explore the nearby forest and tussle with low-level monsters. He can actually *leave his country*, traveling from his hometown of Truce to Porre, a town on the southern continent, to go carousing in a café. There is no sense of story urging him onward, no clear path to the next objective.

Even when this foray into tourism is done, there's ample time to play. The fair itself is loaded with mini-games. The most casual of players could dedicate hours to grinding with Gato, the karaoke fightbot, earning cash to spend at the creepy sideshow tent, where a wager of 80 coins can get Crono's probably already struggling little family another cat. And then cat food. Then more cat food. Which makes more cats, of course. In fact, you could doom Crono's mother to be a pet hoarder by proxy long before you ever discover that *Chrono Trigger* involves time travel. Before you finally step through that time gate and leave Crono's mom alone with the seven cats you just had to have.

•

After completing *Chrono Trigger* in 1995, I wanted to keep adventuring through new worlds like it. But *Chrono Trigger* ended up becoming Square's last hurrah of high fantasy in North America in the 16-bit era. *Secret of Evermore*, released a few months after *Chrono Trigger*, was not the kind of turn-based RPG I was waiting for. It even failed as a follow-up to 1993's action RPG *Secret of Mana*, to which it was a spiritual sequel. And March 1996's *Super Mario RPG*, while cute and innovative, was far from the fantasy that I craved. Square's Super Nintendo golden age was at its end.

Final Fantasy VII changed everything. Gone were the fat clunky cartridges I had to spank and blow in to make cooperate. *FF7* spanned three PlayStation discs. Square had taken a leap into the future, and so had the series. The industrial revolution in *Final Fantasy VI* had given rise to a science fiction adventure in *FF7*. Sure, there were magic and chocobos, but now they competed with gun-arms and helicopters. The familiar little character sprites were here too, but their bodies bulged with excess polygons.

As I trudged through the uncanny valley of *Final Fantasy VIII*—released in my final year of high school—I felt the effects of Square's spell on me starting to dissipate. Maybe it was a fluke. Maybe Square just dropped the ball with this hyper-realistic, over-pretty game. By the time I got to *Final Fantasy IX*, released during my first semester of college, the magic was gone. I felt ready to move on. In college I had little time for RPGs. Those hours of cola-fueled role-playing had been replaced by occasional spurts of *Super Smash Bros.* while binge drinking with friends. Perhaps I had outgrown Square—I was an adult after all, and video games are children's toys, right?

After graduating college, I found myself teaching English halfway across the world in that mecca of mes, Japan. I ended up in a budget, backwater Fukushima City. Fukushima was years away from rising to prominence in the news, and before I took the job there, the only information I'd had on Fukushima was some tourism websites, a Wikipedia entry, and a rough estimate of its proximity to Tokyo. I had imagined the stereotypically frenetic metropolitan Japan that Westerners tend to think of—streets ablaze in neon, with garish cartoon mascots adorning every other building. Fukushima was decidedly *not that*.

Still, I grew comfortable there, made friends, fell in love a few times, and somehow managed to work far less than my fellow alumni stuck eternally in the past. Well, twelve hours behind me, at least. Post-college life was supposed to be my first taste of "the real world," but Japan was far from "real" for me. It was an extended vacation, a chance to satisfy my 21-year-old wanderlust. For many of my foreign colleagues, Japan was even more of a fantasy realm—they jumped into anime, manga, cosplay. They gamed.

I had a lot of free time, and as the weather grew colder, I found myself indoors more often than not. I read every English book that my small group of friends collectively owned, watched every VHS tape of *The X-Files* that had been inexplicably left in my apartment by a previous tenant. I was getting bored. I noticed, though, that the Game Boy Advance I had brought to

Japan was gathering dust in the closet. Maybe I'd buy a Japanese game and use it to improve my language skills. I could make this children's toy educational. *Adult.*

I picked up something familiar but altogether alien—the Japanese Game Boy Advance cartridge of *Mother 1+2* (perhaps better known to us North Americans as *EarthBound Zero+EarthBound*). As I walked through the now Japanese streets of Onett, it all came to me in a flash—*this is what I had been missing!* Square and I had gone our separate ways. They had transformed RPG characters from little collectible figurines into complex intractable mannequins. I wanted more of what used to be. But *new.*

And now, back in the United States, playing through *Chrono Trigger* again, I was afraid. Afraid that playing the game some eighteen years later would ruin the magic. I approached with caution, reaching my hand down gingerly into that abyss of murky memory, wondering if the old abracadabra still had any kick. I can assure you, reader, that there's still plenty of rabbit left in that old hat.

•

If you're reading this book, then you probably still know the magic words. Maybe your memories of the game, like mine had been, are enveloped by the twin mists of *nostalgia* and *getting older*—an expanse of known landmarks hazily illuminated within dark, forgotten patches. There are far more skilled summarists than me, so rather than reproduce the herculean labors already completed by Chrono wiki compilers, let's take a moment to go over the basics.

Crono, a teenage boy from a small town, his techno-savvy gal pal Lucca, and princess-in-disguise Marle end up opening a hole in space-time—a *gate*. Discovering the link between their own era and others, the trio travels through different times assembling a party of allies: the knight-errant-turned-frog, Frog; stalwart robot Robo; rough-and-tumble cavewoman Ayla; and finally Magus, a dark sorcerer with mysterious allegiances. Learning that their planet—that all life itself!—will be destroyed by Lavos, a sinister force from beyond, the septet travel onward, gathering clues and materials, meeting supporters, and defeating foes to prepare themselves for that final, decisive battle for the future.

The plot is deceptively simple. Condensed even further, it might read as a personal ad in some questfinder's forum: *Unlikely hero to save world from cataclysm. Seeks motley assortment of companions. Sidequests guaranteed.*

Underneath the surface and the stock RPG trappings of *Chrono Trigger* are gates into other places and ideas. Many of these gates lead into our world and its curious intersections of cultural understanding. Others lead into different realms of fantasy. Still others are traps, rabbit holes that one can tumble down indefinitely until the real world seems like a wonderland.

I hope this book becomes a key item for you—a *Gate Key*—that unlocks new ideas and views into the rich worlds within and behind the world of *Chrono Trigger*. An epic adventure awaits.

Just press start when you're ready.

THE STRONG,
SILENT TYPE

THE VESSEL WE OPERATE THROUGH the majority of *Chrono Trigger* is a spiky redheaded teenager. It'll be a long way until we ride a vehicle, and even longer before we pilot an actual time machine. So, just who is this dude into whom our start button transports us?

Apparently, not much of anybody.

It's clear that people are invested in Crono's life, like his mother and his bestie Lucca. People around town seem to recognize him. Sometimes. How could they *not*? He's the redheaded pineapple-haired sword-swinging kid from around the corner. It's hard to envision a world where someone like that is forgettable, especially when a vast majority of the people who inhabit *Chrono Trigger* are just so damn interchangeable.

Despite his standout sense of style, Crono isn't much of a *character*. We know that Crono engages in conversations with people, but we don't get to hear—well, *read*—exactly what he says to them. We the players are supposed to be the presence behind Crono, with a press of the A button serving as our conversation starter. Besides occasional chances to advance the dialogue with binary choices, all we can do is tell Crono where to move and how to fight.

In fact, when we are given the chance to "speak" as Crono, the choices aren't even presented in quotation marks. We're not really indicating what Crono says verbatim, but rather, what he *intends* to say. These choices don't even advance the narrative profoundly. We can repeat an "incorrect" response over and over until we finally choose the game-sanctioned answer, or we can pick among two options that only affect the immediate response with no far-reaching repercussions. Rather than making us identify with Crono as a character, our speech choices often remind us how little of what we say actually matters. So do we give a damn about Crono?

As it turns out, we do.

•

I grew up in a nuclear family that slowly and steadily fissioned. By the time I was really aware of myself and my surroundings, my father was already working long weeks away from home, returning on occasional weekends. These weekends became less frequent until they were almost nonexistent, as he traveled farther from home for better opportunities for our family. Boston. Jacksonville. Guadalajara. Malabo. Shenzhen.

My mother was a married single parent, and acted as the sole caretaker for me, my older sister, and later on, that cat I just had to have. I was as blissfully unaware of her struggles as I was selfishly indulgent in video games.

As a thirteen-year-old playing *Chrono Trigger*, I saw myself in Crono. I wanted to be this boy with the encouraging mom and happy little cat who vanished from the small world he inhabited. I fantasized—as most children must and many adults still do—of a catalyst for adventure, of a portal to a new life opening up. Of the universe waking me up into a fateful day.

Pouring myself into Crono was an exercise in projection, of making myself fit. Game designer and lecturer Petri Lankoski has described this type of interaction with our player characters (PCs) as *empathic engagement*. When we begin to see our characters as a reflection of ourselves, we empathize with them. As we control Crono's movements, we are almost literally walking in his shoes. Before games became more complex, dynamic, and story-driven, however, it was not empathy but rather *goal-related engagement* through which we became those little sprites on the screen.

Goal-related engagement describes how closely our gameplay objectives align with our PC—in this case, Crono. Our mission and Crono's are ostensibly the same—defeat the bad thing and save the good thing. It's a simple goal, one that underpins many game narratives spanning every genre. What does Mario in *Super Mario Bros.* want? To defeat the villain and save the princess. What does Link in *The Legend of Zelda* want? Ditto. And while "saving the princess" may seem a very specific, old-fashioned, and gender-biased goal, if we replace "princess" with other words, *bigger* words—"town," "world," "universe!"—we'll find that many games follow the same narrative path from start to finish, regardless of the intricacies of their plots.

The completion of these big goals often coincides with the end of the game. Once Mario defeats Bowser and saves Peach—*Princess Toadstool*, if I'm being textually faithful to my North American experience— the game is over. Once Link topples Ganon and saves Zelda, we're done. There is no post-game for our PCs.

Chrono Trigger complicates this dynamic by offering us the illusion of a post-game—multiple variants on the main ending along with several special ones. Obtaining any of these new endings, however, is *not* aligned with Crono's goal. He sets out to defeat an ancient evil—not see what happens after, or see how a web of choices complicates this outcome. We players, then, have goals beyond those outlined for our PC. We want the achievement of unlocking those endings. We want *bragging rights*.

But Crono doesn't want these. Or does he? At the Millennial Fair, Marle comments on Crono's predilection for carnival games: "You're awfully competitive, aren't you, Crono?" Of course, Marle has just met this stoic boy, but still she seems to know more about him than we do. So is Crono a brash, headstrong punk? A timid, polite youth? That's for us to choose. We are the hero behind Crono, and how we project ourselves onto him makes each player's journey through *Chrono Trigger* unique.

•

The Hero's Journey is an analytical framework that is both useful and biased. The Journey is based on a pattern of narrative milestones first identified by mythologist Joseph Campbell, who in turn was heavily influenced by the work of psychologist Carl Jung. Jung's most well-known archetypes are familiar concepts to many storytellers and their audiences: shadow, animus, anima. The very names bespeak unfathomable depths of symbolism. Using Jungian concepts to catalogue and analyze world mythologies, Campbell articulated the monomyth—or "hero-journey"—a seventeen-step fundamental structure, which he summarized succinctly:

> A hero ventures forth from the world of common day into a region of supernatural wonder: fabulous forces are there encountered

and a decisive victory is won: the hero comes back from this mysterious adventure with the power to bestow boons on his fellow man.

Several of Campbell's mythic checkpoints have almost alchemical names. The Belly of the Whale. The Master of Two Worlds. This "hero-journey" has been further distilled by several writers, often as an abbreviated series of steps with the spruced-up title The Hero's Journey. Some of these new reconfigurations have similarly arcane steps. The Dark Night of the Soul. The Theft of the Elixir. Whether or not Campbell's model accurately applies to all mythologies is debatable, and the adapted Hero's Journey may prove problematic as well. So take as many grains of salt as needed—take the whole shaker, if you must!—as I attempt to put typical RPG hero Crono in the sandals of a mythological figure and walk him through my own version of The Hero's Journey.

The Journey begins with a Call to Adventure. Crono witnesses Marle disappear through an unexpected warp in the fabric of reality and he is compelled to save her. With Lucca's ability to reproduce the anomaly as a form of Aid from the Supernatural, Crono follows Marle through the rift, a Threshold of Danger leading to an unknown world—the past. Here he meets strong enemies and new helpers, with Lucca joining his team permanently and Frog becoming an ally to the party.

Crono literally begins his walk on The Road of Trials, eventually getting arrested, tried, and sentenced to death. Rescued from the depths of prison by Lucca, Crono and company continue to face challenges, but as their obstacles increase in difficulty, their helpers increase in number.

Eventually the hero must face The Ultimate Ordeal. In videogamespeak, this usually translates to The Final Boss. In *Chrono Trigger*, the final boss is Lavos, an alien parasite that will bring the doom of mankind. Squaring off against Lavos deep in the Ocean Palace in 12,000 BC, this should be our moment of triumph, when we save the world and return home wiser and stronger.

But it's not.

The party finds itself woefully underprepared for Lavos and is defeated miserably. Or maybe they're not, and you unlock a surprise ending—but only if you cheat. No offense to the crafty Aladdins who have summoned that all-powerful Game Genie, but *you're supposed to lose at this point*.

This moment of failure coincides with Crono defying our player-made choices. Without any input from our controller, Crono steps forward to face Lavos alone. Lavos, enraged, blasts Crono with a beam of eldritch light. Crono's body electrifies. As the screen fades to white, a dark, shimmering speck rises from his body. *Is that—is that his soul?*

His body begins to disintegrate, the pixels sloughing off until nothing is left but this tiny hovering speck. It pulsates defiant blue, but then it too fades.

Crono is dead.

•

Wait, what?

Our Hero's Journey ends quite abruptly with the death of the hero. In the middle of the game. *And we don't even need him to come back.* This a huge upset, and literally a game-changer.

Since we are no longer required to have Crono in our battle squad, we can learn previously unavailable triple techs—powerful three-person abilities that combine our characters' individual skills. The event also opens up the road to the endgame itself. We can leave Crono suspended in nothingness and battle Lavos without him, and without figuring out what the title of the game even means.

The comprehensive player in me eventually wanted to experience the ending without Crono, but the first time around I just had to save myself from destruction.

From a practical standpoint, Crono is the powerhouse of the game, having participated in every battle and having gained all those hard-fought experience points. Characters not in our active party, by the way, are awarded 75% of the EXP earned in battle, but there are restrictions on how these points are applied to their leveling up. In short, the characters who battle the most are the strongest. Moreover, without Crono, two thirds of the game's triple techs are inaccessible. He is not only the linchpin of our plot, but the battle system itself.

Besides, I needed to see him come full circle. I needed the *me-in-him* to succeed. So what happens to *Chrono Trigger*'s Hero's Journey when there's no hero to journey anymore?

Well, a new Journey starts, within the first. The player now guides a *collective hero*—the party without Crono—through a mini Journey to save the original hero. The Crono-less team accepts a Call to Adventure to save their erstwhile leader, getting mentorship from the gurus Gaspar and Belthasar on how to attempt this near-impossible resurrection.

Interestingly enough, this feat might have been totally impossible, had story planner Masato Katō gotten his way. Katō had originally planned for Crono to die permanently. The party would have temporarily borrowed a version of Crono from the night before the Millennial Fair, but later returned him to face his inevitable death—perhaps that's why he was already fully dressed at the start of our adventure? The idea was rejected in favor of a happier ending, one necessitating a new sidequest.

Saving Crono is an interesting mission, full of parody, titular repetition, and—ugh, fine—a *mini-game*. Unless we spent a lot of time dicking around at the Millennial Fair, kicking robot butt and underage-gambling on foot races, we may have missed the chance at Norstein Bekkler's Tent of Horrors to win non-feline items like Poyozo Dolls—*Chrono Trigger*'s answer to Furbies—or a life-size, functioning doppelgänger of Crono. This last prize raises some serious questions about the nature of Mr. Bekkler, but his ability to furnish the Crono Clone is crucial to reuniting our party with its leader. We're going to need a body double for one of the most important switcheroos in RPG history.

But there is a price for this doll. And it isn't just silver points we can easily earn by ganging up on a singing robot, or by chugging "soda" until we puke. No, we have to play for it. In a timing-heavy match game, players have to compete against the Crono Clone, mimicking his actions—raise the left arm, the right arm, laugh, be surprised. We must accurately imitate the opponent, because if we press the wrong button we lose. As the mini-game progresses, it gets faster and faster. As I frantically mirrored the clone's actions, I found myself reacting to his facial cues, smiling when he laughed, widening my eyes each time he acted surprised.

The skillful player will get this mini-game on the first try. Then there are failures like me. In my most recent replay, I threw the controller at the screen and called the opponent a *goddamn fuckwhore* before I reset the game and tried again. If we had already earned the Crono Clone earlier in the game with Crono at the head of the party, we would have had the interesting experience of imitating the imitation of the PC who is our stand-in. Wow, meta.

Along with the clone, our party also needs the eponymous Chrono Trigger, which Gaspar describes thusly: "It is pure potential. By unleashing a specific course of events, it can have a powerful effect on time." Belthasar adds an additional qualification to the Trigger's ability to restore life—the person who died "must be important to the space-time continuum."

With both the clone and the Chrono Trigger in tow, our party must climb Death Peak, a previously inaccessible and dangerous location complete with several minibosses. These enemies, though, are not the party's ultimate ordeal—activating the Chrono Trigger is. There is a chance it could fail if Crono isn't as important to the universe as our party believes. It would be a huge disappointment to find that the Trigger doesn't fire when pulled. Crono *has* to be important, right?

Depending on who is in our party, we can witness a variety of emotional pleas to the universe to bring Crono back. Their supplications must work, because we are brought to that slice of space-time where Crono hangs in the clutches of Lavos's sinister light. Exchanging his body with the Crono Clone, our heroes pull Crono back into the world of the living.

Crono, resurrected, can continue his original Hero's Journey along with the party. What we thought was the final battle against Lavos was really just another compound step along Crono's Hero's Journey—a Descent into the Abyss followed by a Resurrection from the Dead. Crono and his party can resolve sidequests and obtain powerful weapons until they are prepared for the *real* Ultimate Ordeal of Lavos. If they succeed, they can return heroic through the Threshold of Danger to their ordinary world.

•

As the Journey has been an oft-used tool in storytelling and screenwriting, it has been linked with the classical Aristotelian three-act structure of drama: a setup, a story arc filled with character development and increasing action, and a final act of climax and resolution. Our battle with Lavos should be the best marker for the climax—*it's the battle we're supposed to win*. But we don't, and we are left with a dead Crono and a broken party. And the story itself breaks apart. It can become a swift retaliation against Lavos for murdering Crono, or it can be a meandering journey of ignoring our dead friend while clearing unconnected sidequests. Obviously Aristotle didn't see this one coming.

Game Design Forum founder Patrick Holleman, approaching *Chrono Trigger* from a gameplay perspective, divides the story into two acts punctuated by Crono's demise and its direct aftermath—the linear "Tragedy of the Entity," and the open-worlded "Comedy of the Sages." The first act is an adventure game that creates the illusion of choice and the ability to affect events through time. The second half, a game of puzzles and nonlinear sidequests, makes this power to change history a reality. Holleman's bipartite structure echoes the first English strategy guide, *Chrono Trigger Player's Guide*, which offers the reader a "Chart of Steps" and a "Chart of Events," with Crono's death as the fulcrum.

RPG players usually expect an important character to die, perhaps even a party member whom we directly control. These tragedies equip the party with fresh resolution and sometimes new skills and items to pass through the next obstacle. But to rob the party of its leader in such an abrupt way—*and to allow you to accept this fact without any required response*—is a ballsy move, and one that defies traditional story structures.

Most games couldn't suddenly axe their main characters and expect players to stick with them. *Chrono Trigger*, however, manages to get away with this. The sheer novelty of having the main party member die, of course, isn't enough to keep the player involved. It is the power of the characters who surround, support, and ultimately save Crono that allows the adventure to continue. And in a game where the hero has a hard time speaking up, we're lucky we have friends who have something to say.

PARTY LIKE IT'S 1999 AD

LET ME THROW SOMETHING OUT there—I'm terrible at making friends.

It's not that I don't have friends, or that I'm a bad friend to the ones I do have. I just tend to limit my main party to a few select people I trust to accompany me through life's important journeys. The many acquaintances who pop in and out of my life are valuable NPCs—people who provide me with rich information, surprise bonuses, and quest prompts. But they are not usually the people I call upon when I am in need.

You can choose your friends, but you can't choose your family. A well-known adage that emphasizes the primacy of kinship—of bloodlines and marriage—over friendship. In *Chrono Trigger*, though, we don't even get a choice in our friends.

Besides our taciturn avatar Crono, there are five major heroes who join our party no matter what we do—and no, I haven't forgotten *him*. Sit tight. Like it or not, these five become our extended family for the course of the game, bound by a common interest in saving the world. And if we accept that friendship is something we choose, then the main cast of characters of *Chrono Trigger* are not exactly *friends*. But neither are they *family*—most of them have their own family drama to deal with. Rather, they are something that is neither and both of these things.

They are our fellowship, our *party*—the people who will literally follow us to the end of time.

•

The five characters who answer the call of heroism are an odd and interesting lot. Each has a particular type of weapon that only he or she can equip, and each has an innate affinity for one of four elements: lightning, water, fire, and shadow—*non-alignment* itself is an unofficial fifth element. These weapons and affinities do not simply add variety and strategic challenges to the game, but also complement our party members' characterizations.

The first person to join our crew is Marle, a crossbow-wielding girl and a bit of a gigglepuss. This bubbly adventure-seeker spares no time in sizing up Crono as a potential boyfriend, making him escort her through the Millennial Fair. It might be easy to label Marle—secretly Princess Nadia of Guardia in disguise—as a "tomboy," as a gossipy matron at the fair does. But this oversimplifies Marle into a troubling stereotype, and she's already burdened with the "royal disguised as pauper" trope. Marle does indeed become a romantic interest for commoner Crono, though it might be more accurate to say *he* becomes one for *her*.

Marle's elemental affinity is water. Water nurtures, and is a basic physical need for humans. Marle's healing techniques prove crucial in early battles. Water is also a symbol of sorrow, of tears. Many tender moments in *Chrono Trigger* involve Marle—if we bring her to Death Peak to rescue Crono from time-stasis, we are shown a truly emotional scene of Marle's deep affection for him.

Crono's other major emotional interest is Lucca, a sort of big sister type. Rather than creating a love triangle between Crono, Marle, and Lucca, *Chrono Trigger* not only has Lucca accept Marle unconditionally, but also shows her complimenting Crono for having landed a "cutie."

Lucca is a gifted inventor (or, *inventress*, as the DS version genders it), so her alignment with the element fire—the spark of passion and creativity—is an appropriate choice. While her inventions have a reputation around town for being kooky, she is clearly a genius. Lucca is also an expert marksman (or, *markswoman*, as nobody ever genders it), and her long-range firearms mirror Marle's crossbows.

Crono's journey really begins with the malfunctioning of Lucca's teleportation device, but this only occurs after the introduction of Marle's mystic pendant. This clash of science and magic prefigures the powerful Antipode double techs that these two characters will eventually activate by fusing their water and fire affinities. We should note that the net elemental effect of these Antipode spells creates shadow, the opposite of Crono's element. The original North American release obscures this fact—first localized as "lightning," Crono's element is "light" in the DS translation. The accidental collaboration between Crono's two shadow-animas literally unlocks the gate to adventure.

More specifically, a gate to the Middle Ages, where we meet the aptly-monikered Frog. A chivalrous batrachanthrope and sword-wielding knight, Frog speaks in a "Ye Olde Englishy" dialogue that is as charming as it is grammatically suspect. No one else in 600 AD talks like Frog. Not even Glenn, the boy Frog used to be. We can therefore forgive Frog for having no idea how to use Middle English pronouns properly—it's likely an affectation intended to support his yearnings for heroism.

Because everything about our slimy green swordsfrog simply oozes *hero*.

As squire Glenn, Frog and the legendary knight Cyrus—sworn protector of the royal family, King Guardia XXI and Queen Leene—track down and reclaim the stolen Hero Medal, an emblem of courage.

Later, the two knight-sleuths face the villain Magus in the Denadoro Mountains. Even with the legendary sword Masamune by his side, Cyrus is slain by Magus. The Masamune is broken, and the ensorcelled Glenn plummets to the ground thoroughly transfrogrified by Magus's magic. Glenn, now Frog, manages to recover the lower half of the Masamune along with the Hero Medal, seeking to fill Cyrus's big shoes with his webbed feet.

Frog's most noteworthy weapon is that very same broadsword, which will eventually receive a massive upgrade. But in order to encourage Frog to find his inner hero, we need to make the Masamune whole again. After recovering the upper blade of this sword-that-was-broken, the party commissions guru Melchior to reforge the weapon. At the Magic Cave, Crono does not hand Frog the intact Masamune—he drives it into the ground. Here Aragorn's broken sword Narsil becomes King Arthur's Excalibur, as Frog reenacts the drawing of the sword from the stone. And why shouldn't there be an Excalibur? The upper echelon of Guardia's royal army is, after all, the "Knights of the Square Table."

The animated full motion video (FMV) that accompanies this scene in later editions shows grass rushing in the winds under a darkened sky. This imagery melds perfectly with how I experience "Frog's Theme." The battle drums insist on an onward march, the sweet lonely woodwinds hint at triumph and tragedy. A hero stands ready in lush highlands on the verge of a storm, cape fluttering in the gale as his sword *fwhings* from its sheath! This is questing music.

Although his amphibious form is half of his charm, we can eventually choose to free Frog from his curse—a difficult choice that we will delay for the time being. As an amphibian, Frog's natural element is water. This is also a practical game design choice. Frog's tongue-lashing Slurp technique, while probably pretty gross to experience firsthand, quickly replaces Marle's crucial water-based healing techs after she has vanished from the timeline. Both heavyhitter and caretaker, Frog was one of my most used characters.

Continuing and mercifully ending the sequence of way-too-obvious names, is Robo. *Hint: He's a robot.* Transported to the dark future of 2300 AD, our party discovers him in disrepair. In a scene that reminded me of the eerie 1985 film *Return to Oz*, Lucca repairs the machine-man, who greets her with polite surprise. If I had had the foresight or character space to rename Lucca to "Dorothy," then Robo would have made a fine "Tik-Tok."

We will much later learn that Robo has a tragic background, but he first functions as an object of Lucca's desires. Much like how Marle fixates on ensnaring Crono, and how Frog yearns to become Cyrus—realized heteronormatively as a desire to *protect Queen Leene*—Lucca needs someone upon whom to inscribe her passions. She establishes a direct physical connection with Robo as his resurrector (or, *resurrectrix*, if you *really* want to), and soon as his regular maintenance person.

Robo reveals his serial number to be R-66Y, but we will discover that his true name is Prometheus. In an ironic twist on the Greek myth, the fire-affinitied Lucca brings the spark of life to Robo. Robo is implied to be male, despite a lack of reproductive organs. He certainly doesn't balk at others referring to him with the masculine pronoun. Since romance also applies to robots in *Chrono Trigger*, Robo has his own probably-female love interest, Atropos XR. In Greek mythology—you really should have studied up before playing!—Atropos was one of the Three Fates, goddesses who controlled human destiny by spinning, measuring, and cutting the threads of life allotted to each mortal. Atropos had the honor of being the final snipper, and *Chrono Trigger*'s Atropos XR is similarly an agent of human demise, despite her cute pink paint job and adorable little ribbon.

Some of the humor in Robo's dialogue comes from his confessed inability to grasp human emotions fully—a fact which is blatantly false. Like many other beloved androids in popular culture, Robo *does* know what love is. If we bother with the endgame sidequests, Robo must eventually battle and destroy a reprogrammed

Atropos XR, leaving him alone in the world except for Lucca. Once we defeat Lavos and correct the timeline, however, we will see Atropos XR and Robo together as a happy couple.

In that very same sidequest, we learn that before his breakdown, Robo had been sent by the supercomputer Mother Brain to study humans and their weaknesses. Square has used the "party member as traitor" trope effectively in other titles, but in *Chrono Trigger* this nugget of information comes far too late in the game to be of any real import. Rather than give Robo any additional depth, the unspooled plot thread of his potential treachery only reminds us that Robo's storyline could have used a bit more polish.

Last in the regular roster is cavewoman Ayla, a blast from the past in all senses of the phrase. Like Robo, Ayla has no elemental alignment. A prehistoric party girl, she revels in the physical. She eats, drinks, sleeps, and fights hard. She probably does other things hard, but this is best left to the players' imaginations.

Upon first meeting her, the party is exasperated at her inability to understand the concept of time travel. Here, the golden-haired Ayla might be dangerously close to the "dumb blonde" stereotype. Except that she's the most put-together of anyone in our party. She has a steady partner, she's the chief of her tribe, and eventually she'll be the leader of all early humans. Noble in battle even to her enemies, Ayla always chooses courage over fear. She is also incredibly pragmatic: "Ayla fight while alive! Win and live. Lose and die. Rule of life. No change rule." Powerful Ayla and her submissive boyfriend Kino will establish the bloodlines that eventually become the royal lineage of Guardia. Though this fact only becomes apparent in the ending, Marle will have battled alongside her distant grandmother for a good portion of the story.

We can finish the game with only these five characters—or six, if we really do care about that chatterbox Crono. The observant player, however, will notice an open slot in the menu's party window. Room enough for a seventh character.

•

As far as hidden characters go, Magus is hiding in plain sight. As in, directly in your field of vision.

The instruction manual included with the initial Super Nintendo release in North America makes no mention of Magus as a potential PC. Similarly, the early spoiler-light Japanese guide, *Kurono Torigā Kōryaku Daitokushū*—or, the *Chrono Trigger Strategy Big Special*, if you want to get a good feel for how awkwardly Japanese directly translates to English—does not include Magus in the introductory lineup of characters. In fact, the guide emphasizes the role of Magus as an antagonist. But, much like many a feline from Norstein Bekkler's Tent of Horrors, the cat must have gotten out of the bag pretty quickly. Later strategy guides in Japanese and English do not attempt to surprise the player with Magus, but rather openly advertise him as a regular party member.

After the fall of the Kingdom of Zeal in 12,000 BC, the careful shopper will notice a curiously unequippable scythe now available for purchase in the Last Village. Unlike finding the reclusive sasquatch Umaro and gender-ambiguous tatterdemalion Gogo in *Final Fantasy VI*, tracking down the character who can wield this weapon is not a difficult task. In fact, confronting Magus is a required story event. But there's a twist.

We can choose to fight Magus and finally give him the ass-whooping he deserves. If said ass does indeed get whooped, the curse he laid upon the young squire Glenn will be broken, returning him to his handsome, emerald-haired human form. But this is not a reward we get until the very, very end: The human Glenn is not playable in *Chrono Trigger*.

For players like me who consider hidden characters essential, we have the option to swallow our pride, buckle our ass-whooping belts, and make peace with Magus. Frog will quite maturely note that killing Magus will not bring back his long-dead friend Cyrus. At this point, we might wonder why we can't just go back to the past with our awesome time machine to rescue and recruit Cyrus. Moving on.

Refusing to fight Magus will unlock him as a character. In a game with a somewhat limited selection of PCs, there is little reason not to recruit Magus. And whether we kill Magus or have him join us, the ending FMV in later editions suggests that Glenn will indeed be restored to his human form. Unless it is absolutely necessary to see Frog change his sprite briefly at the end of the game, getting Magus is the winning choice. All the strategy guides are pretty much telling us to get him, right?

Magus is, after all, one of the most compelling characters in the game.

•

I've always had a soft spot for antiheroes. Their constant struggle to navigate between the already ill-defined categories of good and evil. Their refusal to assert allegiance to anyone but themselves. Their *humanness*. Magus is, however, less of an antihero than he is an *antivillain*.

Magus first appears as an enemy, looking like he might eventually become the final boss. As his backstory slowly unfolds, his alignment becomes murkier. Wielding the power of shadow, he is elementally opposed to our protagonist. A more accurate translation of Crono's element *ten* is "heaven"—not "light" or "lightning"—and Magus's element shadow is *mei*, a darkness associated with Pluto and Hades—the gloom beyond death.[1] He is an archetypical shadow and bizarro version of Crono. Each has a single mother and a faithful cat, and neither is a great conversationalist. Magus eventually becomes a reluctant ally, a villain who puts his villainy on the backburner to take care of a greater foe. The enemy of my enemy, and all that.

Magus was formerly Janus, the child of the power-mad Queen Zeal in 12,000 BC. Friends with no one but his cat Alfador and his sister Schala, Magus harbors a darkness that grows with his developing powers. Dropping references to "black winds" and hinting at the imminent death of a party member—namely Crono—Janus is a spooky little dude. Like the Roman deity his English name evokes, Janus has one face he shows the world, and another turned towards the shadows.

Time-orphaned by the awakening of Lavos in 12,000 BC, Janus is hurled forward to the Middle Ages, only to be discovered by the trickster miniboss Ozzie and presumably raised to cultivate his latent magic. By the time our party meets him for the first time in battle, Magus has become the leader of organized monsterkind, along with his generals Flea, Slash, and former foster parent/teacher Ozzie.

---

1   Compare the characters for *ten* (天) and *mei* (冥).

Despite observing the changes that Lavos's all-consuming power wrought upon Queen Zeal, young Prince Janus grows up to become a mirror version of his mother. Bent on acquiring immeasurable power, Magus surrounds himself with powerful but ultimately subservient archminions and builds his own kingdom. In a plot point that parallels the three gurus rebelling against the malevolent Queen Zeal, it is Magus the overlord who eventually turns his back on his three warmonger cronies. But he does not reject the shadow completely—it is his elemental alignment and the source of his power.

Magus is the only PC who has a motive for destroying Lavos that transcends altruism. As noble as the intentions of the other party members are, not one of them has any direct interest in defeating Lavos. By the time Lavos emerges in 1999 AD, all of our human characters will have died, having lived their lives without experiencing the effects of the apocalypse. Ayla is something of an exception, since she and her people will deal with the ice age caused by Lavos's destructive arrival on earth. But this is unpreventable. The party will never get the chance to defeat Lavos before it arrives on earth. As for Robo, he might not even exist if the end of the world is prevented. By agreeing to help topple Lavos, he resigns himself to potential martyrdom.

Magus, however, wants *revenge*. He wants to take down Lavos for stealing his sister—for stealing his *childhood*. Even after defeating Lavos, Magus is still tormented by the memory of Schala, lost in time. In the DS version of *Chrono Trigger*, which adds a new optional boss and an ending to tie the game more directly with sequel *Chrono Cross*, Magus—at least some version of Magus from one timeline or another—finally discovers Schala. She has become half-captive, half-absorbee of Lavos, who it seems was not destroyed, but rather banished somewhere beyond time. Even if we beat this boss, we still end up defeated. Schala warns Magus that his power will not be enough to defeat this new, upgraded Lavos. Demonstrating uncharacteristic awareness of his faults, Magus wipes his own memories and ends up in an unfamiliar place, remembering nothing but a compulsion to find something important to him.

To me, a player of the original Super Nintendo version, this new ending is a big *screw you*. Having our party lose to a boss that we already kind of defeated, and that characters in the sequel are able to defeat, makes it feel like our team—the team that saves the world!—*isn't good enough*. Furthermore, *Chrono Trigger* does not need retconning into an unstable Chronoverse just to answer for the poor choices of its sequel. Worse, this new ending forces Magus—again, *some version of him*, because *Chrono Cross* did all that dimension-hopping business—to choose cowardice over arrogance. Magus is an uncompromisingly egotistical loner, and no matter how strongly his affections toward Schala transcend fraternal love—it's a little weird, right?—sacrificing his memories, *especially* those of his beloved sister, is just not in his character. I much prefer to see him set forth in silence on his quest to save Schala, vanishing into time.

•

All of Crono's allies have their own roles to play in our journey, and any of them are fit to stand up to Lavos in the final battle. The catch, of course, is that we can only choose three.

RPGs that feature large, customizable parties generally force us to leave a few characters out of the fray of battle. There are good reasons for this from a game design standpoint—maintaining a delicate balance of powers in battle, or fitting the constraints of the screen display. Rarely do games offer explanations for limitations on party size. Why, for example, should only four characters in *Final Fantasy VI* go questing while the other ten laze around an airship? It seems ludicrous that such an assemblage of heroes wouldn't all just go out and kick monster ass in a squad thirteen strong. Do we really need more than one hero on guard duty lest our ride gets jacked?

Chrono Trigger gives us plausible, if flimsy, excuses each time. When Marle is rescued in 600 AD from the world of neither death nor life that the demise of her ancestor paradoxed her into, we are left with a quartet of Marle, Crono, Lucca, and Frog. But then Frog sets off on his own, too ashamed of his failure to protect the Queen. There goes that party of four.

Later (of course it's "later"), in 2300 AD, Crono, Marle, and Lucca recruit the newly repaired Robo. Here game-design-as-story rears its head again. Someone needs to remain in the Proto Dome while the others go turn on the power elsewhere. Because that one crucial door will remain sealed unless someone manually opens it. *Of course*. With the temperamental door opened, the four stumble upon a gate. It leads to what appears to be an oversized broom closet, but is actually the End of Time, the nexus of infinity.

Why do we wind up at the End of Time? Because when more than three people travel through gates simultaneously, time goes all wonky or something. Of course it does. So, why don't people just travel through gates one at a time? It certainly works at the end of the game when Lucca's *gate to everywhere* sends everyone back to their respective homes. Whatever.

Then, even later (actually "much earlier") in 65,000,000 BC, there are only enough dactyls to carry three party members to the Tyrano Lair to defeat the enemies of early humanity. Despite the fact that later, these same three dactyls support *four* people—Crono, Ayla, her beau Kino, and our third party member.

And when we finally get our time machine, the Epoch, why, of course it's a three-seater! Assuming that we save Crono from a fate presumably worse than death—perhaps the same nullness that Marle had been grandfathered into—and that we recruit Magus, we eventually have more allies hanging out at the End of Time than we do in the active party. And all of them are itching to accompany us!

It's a real shame that we can't send out the entire team to take down enemies with screen-clearing, seizure-inducing, panelemental septuple techs. Such ultra-powerful moves, though, would probably considerably change the dynamics of play to which we have grown accustomed.

When we play games like *Chrono Trigger* we either tacitly accept their rules—incoherent as they may seem—or we don't play at all.

•

Let me throw something else out there—I don't understand the rules of friendship. Or if there are even rules when it comes to friends. We learn some fundamental preschool guidelines that happen to work pretty damn well. *Be nice. Share your toys.*

As we become older, we find that these aren't as easy to implement as public television mascots would have us believe. So we supplement them. *Let your guard down*. But never, *Keep your guard down*, right? *Forgive and forget*. Or isn't it sometimes, *Forgive but don't forget?*

And as we get even more mature and more chemically complex, lines between family and friends, friendship and romance, love and sex get drawn, erased, redrawn. And the rules expand and grow nuanced. Sections of the rules beget subsections. And from these, clauses and subclauses. And then the subclauses are quoted as independent, Bartlett-sized quotables. And they clash with other independent truths and fortune cookie aphorisms.

Even with the myriad factors that determine how personalities clash and complement, we have a host of largely immutable qualities that regulate behaviors among individuals and groups. Things like our gender, our sex, our sexuality, our race, our ethnicity, our culture, our language. The rise-above-it-all spirit wants us to believe that these things *just don't matter*. Except they kind of really do. We are at once encouraged to embrace commonalities while simultaneously celebrating differences.

This seems remarkably easy to do in *Chrono Trigger*. Although party members come from different time periods, they are united not only by their desire to defeat

Lavos, but also a static world language and enduring town-based culture. By recruiting robots, frogmen, and scantily-clad cavepeople, our party seems to be a real grab bag of differences. But both on the surface and beneath it, the people of *Chrono Trigger* have a lot more in common than we might realize.

STRAIGHT? WHITE? MALE?

I

KIRITSU!

The voice of a stern gym teacher in his freshly-laundered tracksuit thunders across the gymnasium-now-auditorium, followed by the sound of quick shuffling and shoes squeaking on the hardwood as some 400 students rise from sitting cross-legged. The aging principal plods up on the stage and beams from behind the lectern.

Rei!

The 400 bow in unison, torsos lunging forward in smooth practiced arcs. That strict gym coach could measure these kids with a protractor and hit 45° on each of their backs. The principal greets the children with a booming *Good morning!* Well, closer to *Gude moaning goo*. Some of the students giggle. A few smartasses enthusiastically return the English greeting. Most stand perplexed.

Chakuseki!

The students get back into mock lotus position on the floor and wait. Today is an unusual day for the students of Shinobu Junior High. Many of them have been eying the bearded white guy standing off to the right of the stage, some curiously and some askance.

The principal talks about some goals for the year, peppering uncharacteristic Anglicisms into his schoolmarmish Japanese. His first order of business is to explain who the hell this whiteboy is and what he's doing there. "…*Maikeru Wiriamusu-sensei!*"

That's my cue. My stomach is full of butterflies and instant coffee sludge. I bounce up the stairs, skipping a step to the amazement of a few students. What will these white people do next? The principal shakes my hand, firmly and demonstratively. These kids have just seen an alien land in their gym.

I face the crowd. The staff and faculty flank the entire student body of seventh, eighth, and ninth graders. They are a sea of off-black uniforms, straight black hair, and quizzical brown eyes set in various shades of suntanned faces. They are staring right at me. I take a deep breath and open my mouth.

•

Being a temporary citizen of Fukushima City was my first true taste of feeling like a minority.

Although Caucasians make up the largest minority of the city of Philadelphia, white privilege has given me the luxury of being completely unaffected by this. Growing up in a mostly white pocket of Southwest Philadelphia, many ethnic concerns were *intraracial*. My family still felt the immediate legacy of their immigrant forebears and their competition with other immigrant groups. I often shadowed my father on his many trips to the meeting hall of an Irish-Catholic men's benevolent association—really, a fraternity clubhouse with its own bar. There in the converted printer's shop my great-grandfather used to run, I inhaled the musty scent of what I believed were ancient Celtic artifacts. I heard the lilting brogues of mysterious Irish nationals, some of whom I later learned were Irish Republican Army sympathizers and probably even abettors. I choked down ham and cabbage with terrorists, and I was none the wiser.

I was educated at Catholic schools from grades one through twelve. Families who could afford the tuition sent their kids there for semi-affordable private education, regardless of which gods they rooted for. Education and plurality were intertwining, inseparable experiences for me. Regardless of our ethnocultural backgrounds, we were united in restrictive, unbreathable clothing—tight navy ties on mock Oxford shirts, and over these mocksfords, itchy midnight-blue sweaters.

So four years after taking off my Catholic uniform for the last time, I stood before the student body of Shinobu, stumbling over my mirror-rehearsed self-introduction in Japanese, codeshifting clumsily from the familiar tone to the honorific, wondering why this scene felt both uncannily similar to my school days and yet so profoundly different. And all the while the silent horde of ethnosimilar students in their neat uniforms stood with their brass-plated nametags glinting in the sunlight. Just where the hell was I?

•

The ethnic pie chart of Japan is only half-baked. The Japanese census does not, like the United States' questionnaire, ask for ethnic self-identification, but rather legal nationality—*kokuseki*. Therefore, a misinterpretation of the statistic that Japan consists of 98.5% "Japanese" and 1.5% "other" suggests that Japan is a good deal more racially homogenous than it actually is. Walking through the streets of Fukushima, however, one might wonder where that other 1.5% is hiding.

The scarcely populated world of *Chrono Trigger* is inhabited by one global monorace, spanning all the way from prehistory to the dismal future of 2300 AD. NPCs are differentiated largely by clothing design and occasionally with palette swaps—Crono's mother, for instance, is one variation of a female villager type from both the Middle Ages and the present day. It's refreshing to see a culture with a far less fickle sense of fashion. Regardless of what they wear, or the outlandish color of their hair, every unambiguously human being in *Chrono Trigger* has fair skin. Even the official character art of the game shows only subtle variations in skin tone.

Monsters in *Chrono Trigger* demonstrate a much more pluralistic view of racial relations. Transported through a gate in Medina Village, 1000 AD, our party surprises the two imps who reside there—one a cerulean "blue imp," the other a dark mustard "mud imp." The relationship between these two is not clear, but the mud imp scolds the interlopers: "Who do you think you are? Coming and going out of our closet at all hours." They are clearly housemates, possibly a couple. They offer our human party some food before sending them on their way. There aren't even *interspecies* tensions at this little bed and breakfast!

Indeed, many monsters in *Chrono Trigger* seem to be functionally post-racial, while the humans that they coexist with, and are occasionally massacred by, are helplessly *non-racial*. The only evidence of any variant ethnicity in humanity is the mingling of the rust- and yellow-haired Iokan tribe with the purple-haired Larubans in 65,000,000 BC—all of whom are the same skin color. When these tribes eventually unite under Ayla, they intermarry, creating a single race whose major feature is unpredictable shades of hair.

This lack of human diversity did not strike the me of 1995 as odd. It was simply an aesthetic tied to the games I loved to play. I was certainly aware that games—even RPGs—could and *did* represent a multitude of skin colors to increase sprite variation. *EarthBound*, for instance, has some dark-skinned NPCs. One well-used sprite, "Mohawk Man," always reminded me of Mr. T. It would take Square a few more years and yet another "final" fantasy game to unveil Barret Wallace, their own answer to the beloved bouncer-turned-actor-turned-fool-pitier.

But *EarthBound* was the *real world*. Or at least, a fictionalized and heavily distorted simulacrum of our own. Square's fantasy RPGs were faraway planets of majestic kingdoms, mystic crystals, fluffycute moogles, and chocobo farms. And when villagers sat down for a feast of spicy chocobo wings, the only *racial* tensions that would have mattered were *species* tensions. Monster attacks had been increasing lately, hadn't they? It wasn't safe to go out at night anymore, was it? Any number of hackneyed NPC quotes hint at *dangerous others* lurking on the edges of town, ready to strike.

Chrono Trigger embraces a wide range of motifs— prehistoric man-dino clobberfests, futuristic robot-spanking gunfights, turn-of-the-century idyllics. But the theme upon which the classic Square RPG legacy was built is *sword and sorcery*, a genre so pervasive it can be cautiously synonymous with *fantasy*. The further back we travel through Square's catalog of RPGs, the more elements of futurism and technology disappear. The world of the first *Final Fantasy* is almost free of sci-fi elements. Besides the odd robot or two, the world is made of typical fantasy denizens—elves, dwarves, mermaids. And the very first mission that precedes the introductory credits—a sort of prelude adventure—is to *save a goddamn princess!* How much more typical can you get?

The roots of early magic-medieval Square RPGs—let's say *Final Fantasy*, released in 1987—stretch into Japanese ground tilled a year and a half earlier by Enix's *Dragon Quest*, itself inspired by computer RPGs like *Wizardry* and *Ultima*, both released in 1981 on North American soil. These games in turn trace their origins to earlier attempts to make pen-and-paper role-playing games electronic. Perhaps the grandaddiest of these was *Dungeons & Dragons*—a household name even to non-gamers. *D&D* drew on mechanics from already established miniature wargames and added fantastic elements from a wide variety of mythologies and speculative fiction. And although *D&D* developer Gary Gygax claimed the similarities of his game to J.R.R. Tolkien's *Lord of the Rings*-centric legendarium to be superficial—yes, there are *hobbits* (er, "halflings") in *Dungeons & Dragons*—he did note that he borrowed those elements *deliberately* to reach a wider audience, one that was at the time absolutely mad for hobbits.

So what? Well, we can now position *Chrono Trigger* as a descendant—a distant great-grandnephew?—of a game that directly appropriated iconic elements from *Lord of the Rings*. And Tolkien and his drinking buddy C.S. Lewis, the creator of Narnia, weren't just writing novels for entertainment. In fact, cultural theorist and digital media specialist Tanner Higgin contends that they were creating new European mythologies, using fantasy worlds as surrogates for Western Europe, with the metarace *human* substituting for whites. Nonhuman races and evil-aligned humans in Tolkien's Middle-Earth, then, were the dangerous, nonwhite others who occupied lands outside of the Eurosphere. It's no mere coincidence that popular cinematic adaptations of *Lord of the Rings*—and contemporary fantasy franchises like Harry Potter and Game of Thrones—rely on Eurocentrism as their cultural touchstone.

Are the humans of *Chrono Trigger* "white"? They kind of looked that way to the 1995 version of me. It was easy for me to see Crono's light peachy face and project my own onto him. The lack of other distinct skin tones in Crono's community suggested that these people were all of the same race. But to players in Japan who experienced *Chrono Trigger* months before I could, these light-skinned characters could have easily been Asian. Regardless of impossible hair colors.

•

Far-out physical features—Lucca's lavender hair, for instance—hint that *game humans* are not quite the same as *player humans*. But their overall design implies that these humans are *supposed to be us*. Such exoticizations of character design achieve an aesthetic commonly called *mukokuseki*, or "nationalitilessness." *Mukokuseki* is the absence of *kokuseki*, which some of you may remember is the Japanese census's answer to the North American question of "ethnicity." The conflation of "nationality" with "ethnicity" makes *mukokuseki* a difficult term to tackle—is this an absence of citizenship, or ethnic identity, or both?

Kōichi Iwabuchi, a professor of media and cultural studies who introduced the term to English discourse, notes that *mukokuseki* is an attempt to remove the "cultural odor" of Japan from international products. But anyone familiar with Japanese manga, anime, and video games can see past the green coiffures and fuschia eyebrows and *smell* the Japaneseness. In an interview included in *Kurono Torigā Kōryaku Daitokushū*, art designer Akira Toriyama of Dragon Ball series fame specifically states that he intended to create a *mukokuseki* cast of characters for the various eras of *Chrono Trigger*.[2] One of Toriyama's *Dragon Ball Z* characters—the jet-black, big-lipped Mr. Popo—would later be recolored blue after his poorly-received North American anime debut. Subculture critic Tetsu Misaki writes that even some Japanese protest groups judged this character as offensive.

While *mukokuseki* might be an attempt to make Japanese goods more desirable in the international marketplace, Toriyama's design choice for Mr. Popo demonstrates that these efforts can fail miserably when characters veer too close to real-world stereotypes. Toriyama himself might have simply been trying to add variety to an already large cast of *mukokuseki* characters, and the resemblance of Mr. Popo to a blackface caricature could be chalked up to unfortunate coincidence. Nevertheless, Toriyama is not ignorant of how real-world sensibilities influence design. In that same interview, Toriyama reveals that he wanted a protagonist with a katana—something to lend him an "Oriental feel" not present in previous RPGs.[3]

To consider the human character designs from *Chrono Trigger*, then, involves a complex interplay between the fantasy genre's reliance on Euro- and Anglocentric

---

2 "いろんな時代に行くわけですから、ちょっと無国籍な感じのキャラクターにした方がいいかな…"
3 "主人公、日本刀なんか持って東洋的な感じがしますね。普通のRPGとは違う。"

characters as "default humans" and the realities of the game's art design and developmental influences. But a jaunt through Guardia's Millennial Fair still invites the question—*Why is everyone light-skinned?*

II

Watari Junior High is a short bike ride from my more-than-accommodating apartment, though even with a bellyful of heated onigiri from the nearby convenience store, I'm dragging ass. Arriving at school undercaffeinated, I find both refillable Zōjirushi urns in the teacher's room spurting out the last dregs of hot water, making my daily instant coffee sludge more of a thick paste.

I lug the two big urns over to the kitchenette, where the comically oversized kettle has just begun to whistle. The very capable head of the English program—a nervous, tittering, but generally affable man—sidles up to me, informing me with some embarrassment that I don't need to do this. He calls over to a younger female teacher, who enthusiastically takes the kettle from me and refills the urns. I thankpologize to her—I've been confusing *thank you* and *I'm sorry* now that I speak Japanese for more than half of the day—and I offer to make some tea for her with the freshly boiled water. The English teacher praises my "largesse"—he's got an impressive, if sometimes stilted, vocabulary—but reminds me that these domestic matters are usually handled by the female staff.

I usually bring my coffee into a small room accessible from the far corner of the teacher's office, a hidden oasis of soft couches and carcinogens. This is the *kitsuenshitsu*—the smoking room—and it is totally acceptable in a country where cigarettes are sold in prominent public vending machines. Women rarely venture in here. I practice my Japanese with the male teachers through a cloud of burnt tobacco slurry and do some serious backroom cultural exchanges. Topics I would never dream to discuss with my junior high students—drugs, sex customs, average American penis size—are free of taboo in this smoky boy's club.

Once in a while, the artsy-cool music teacher surprises the usual chimneystacks and saunters in with her ultralong slim menthols. The men all bow, apologize, and offer her their seats. It is a comically polite game of musical chairs and misdirected chivalry. I find myself wanting to follow their lead—to be *culturally appropriate*. At the same time, I feel a conflicting desire to raise high the flag of American egalitarianism and treat this woman the same way I'd treat any of the male staff. I half-stand and give her a polite nod-bow as she fills a newly vacated seat.

•

The main cast of *Chrono Trigger* is not exactly a boy's club. Three of the seven PCs are male. This is a definite improvement over *Final Fantasy VI*, whose ensemble cast of fourteen PCs featured only three discernable females.[4] Most early Square RPGs are similarly skewed. And no matter the gender ratios, in all games that have clear protagonists they are always males. The three female heroes of *Chrono Trigger*, though, are a strong bunch—Ayla is in fact cartoonishly strong, a barefisted fighter in a world of weapons—but that doesn't leave them free of gender stereotypes.

Marle is a princess who doesn't need saving—well, except for that one time when she does. Her debut in the game is also quickly accompanied by the introduction of a love story that both heteronormalizes Crono and makes Marle seem like an emotional mess, since we never get to experience the silent Crono returning her affections. This one-sidedness only intensifies as the game progresses. Touching moments—Marle thanking Crono after being rescued from oblivion in 600 AD, or that tear-jerking scene on Death Peak—are made weirdly unbalanced by Crono's insistent unresponsiveness. Marle's genuine emotion starts looking like hysterics.

She also falls victim to Square's tendency to make curative "white mage" characters female. While Marle

_____

4   The mime Gogo's gender is unrevealed.

is not a white mage *per se*—if anything, she is a "water mage"—she performs the function of healer well, having the best defensive and support magic in the game, including the most powerful resurrection spell, Life 2. Although Marle's offensive spells are on par with other characters', her preferred physical attack method is not a melee weapon. Her crossbow works as a bludgeon when she is close to an enemy, but she tends to fire from a distance. Either way, her physical attacks are among the weakest in the game.

These stock genderings notwithstanding, Marle is the game's most headstrong character. She is the only one who willingly rebels against society's high expectations for her, and decides to forge her own path. In doing so, she stands up to the highest authority in the land, the patriarchal monarchy led by her father King Guardia XXXIII. "All I asked was for you to behave like a princess," he reprimands her at Crono's trial, completely oblivious to her feelings for the accused hero. If being a princess means suppressing her true self, Marle wants no part of it.

Lucca, Marle's co-anima to Crono, is another ranged weapon user, and her gun is even weaker than Marle's crossbow. Lucca is also a frequent *dea ex machina* early in the game. Unlike Marle, who propels the early plot onward passively—first by disappearing into time, then by vanishing from it completely—Lucca catalyzes events. It is her telepod that begins the adventure into the past, and her Gate Key that allows Crono and Marle to return safely to 1000 AD. Later, she will save Crono again when he breaks out of prison. Without Lucca we can't repair and recruit Robo, whom we need to open up the End of Time because of that rule of three nonsense. All of these accomplishments are due to Lucca's keen scientific mind.

The field of science, however, has traditionally been dominated by men, especially at the highest levels. In Japan in particular, women in science have been viewed as unattractive. *Unwomanly*. Lucca does indeed perfectly match a stereotype described by journalist Miki Tanikawa—the science girl "whose hair is disheveled and who does not care about beauty." With her frumpy, baggy clothing, asymmetric cap, and Coke bottle glasses that "she could probably see the back side of the moon with,"[5] Lucca is far from the windswept beauty Marle is. Her only in-game romance is her machine-worship of automaton Robo. Later, as the final FMV shows, Lucca has built her own miniature version of Robo after the original has returned to the future to reunite with Atropos XR. The construction of Robo Jr. demonstrates Lucca's quick scientific progress—the observant player will remember that Lucca had first concluded that

---

5   So says a fairgoer at the unveiling of Lucca's telepod.

"two-legged, walking humanoid robots are virtually impossible to create." It seems karaoke addict Gato was a failure on many levels.

The FMV continues to unfold this epilogue for Lucca. As the surrogate Robo—more a child than a *Weird Science*-style lover—totters behind her on a stroll through the woods, Lucca spies a shimmering object. It is a pendant, Schala's pendant in fact—perhaps also Marle's? Whatever the custodial history of this key item, Lucca now finds it attached to a baby. If we have the wherewithal to play through *Chrono Cross*—I didn't— we will learn that not only does this baby become Kid, a major player in the sequel, but will also be Lucca's first surrogate child and the impetus for her to create an orphanage.

I'm on the fence about the Chrono series's decision to push Lucca into the role of single mother. From one angle, it seems to be an easy way to dissociate Lucca from career scientist and recast her in the traditional gender role of stay-at-home mom, one which her own mother Lara fills well. Then again, Lucca, who can either succeed or fail in preventing Lara's partial paralysis, learns from this unique time-travel episode the value of her own mother. It would be unfair to make Lucca choose between motherhood and science, so what does it mean that Lucca accepts the role of everyone's mother? No version of *Chrono Trigger* provides a resolution to this conundrum, but we can hope that the coexistence of Robo Jr. and Kid provides a unique opportunity for Lucca to combine her scientific and familial desires.

The last of our female heroes is Ayla, and boy, does she turn the sex dial up to *fuck*! Toriyama's official artwork shows Ayla's ample breasts filling up her skimpy furs. Unlike the game's other blonde bombshell, Marle, Ayla shows a lot more than just the hint of cleavage—she goes full exposed midriff. While Ayla is undoubtedly the game's *sexiest* character, she is also colored with some decidedly unfeminine tendencies, like hard drinking and unabashed belching. In the first North American translation, all of this boozing is censored to "eating soup." It is unfortunate, however, that a required event in the game is for Crono to outdrink—er, outeat—Ayla at a prehistoric party. Ayla loses with dignity and respect for Crono's capacity—and perhaps, for our ability to press that goddamn A button in rapid succession. Still, I can't help but feel that this is both a joyless mini-game and an undermining of Ayla's fierceness.

Ayla is counterbalanced by Azala, the leader of the reptites—a kind of *dino sapiens* and rival to early mankind. Although ungendered in the Super Nintendo version, the Nintendo DS translation artfully suggests that Azala is female. The clash of these two powerful women for the fate of the planet is a welcome change from predominantly male dyads. Strong female support characters like Azala—hero and villain alike—help diversify images of femininity in *Chrono Trigger*. Queen Zeal, driven mad by vanity and lust for power, is a stark contrast to Mother Brain, whose cold logic dictates the rise of a civilization of robots. As far as we can tell, though, Mother Brain only creates one femmebot—Robo's female companion Atropos XR. Mother Brain's technogynocracy is an interesting parallel to Queen Zeal's royal court, which is similarly all-male except for her daughter Schala. Far less threatening than these two femme fatales but perhaps just as powerful, meek Schala proves instrumental in saving our party from Lavos after Crono is killed. And if we buy what *Chrono Cross* is peddling, Schala will eventually *fuse* with Lavos, becoming the Dream Devourer, the most powerful villain in the Chronoverse.

Unfortunately, the presence of these significant NPCs belies the sheer number of male characters who keep the plot moving forward. For every Azala, there are literally two Ozzies. Men dominate the landscape, and eventually the political structures of organic lifeforms on the planet. They also represent an overwhelming percentage of the NPCs in the game.

Playing through the DS version of *Chrono Trigger*, I counted 425 human characters.[6] Of these, only 154

---

6   I counted all "unique" human NPCs (not double-counting, for example, the survivors in the Last Village in 12,000 BC, who we would have encountered already), all flashback

(35%) are female, while a whopping 266 (61%) are male—and for those of you counting along, the missing five are children from prehistory and from 2300 AD, whose gender is not clearly indicated. Examining these numbers across the major eras during gameplay, prehistory is the most gender-balanced society, with 1.6 men for every woman. Even if we assume the woolly cavekids are all female, men still outnumber women. It will turn out to be 1000 AD that ends up the most evenly distributed, assuming we factor in the Moonlight Parade that occurs during the canonical endings. The parade is literally bursting with women—taking a few steps off the racecourse into the lower square will show female dancers popping out of thin air to twirl in celebration. Little girls raise their arms and faces in song. Of the 33 new NPCs at the parade, 32 are female. Not only are the endings where the Moonlight Parade occurs canonically satisfying, they also provide the most hopeful outlook for gender equality we're going to find in *Chrono Trigger*.

I chose specifically to exclude monsters from the count above. Determining the gender of monsters in the game is a difficult task, though we must assume many monsters are female. The continued existence

characters, and none of the non-canonical ending characters. The three time-displaced gurus were counted as citizens of their home era.

of the monster population in Medina Village in 1000 AD hinges on this crucial fact. Unless most monsters reproduce asexually, which would be no fun at all.

Oh, did someone say "monster sex"? One of the few monsters clearly designated as female is the "naga-ette," which has the lower body of a snake and the bustline of a well-endowed woman. If the party explores the depths of cathedral in 600 AD, we discover "the secret Naga-ette Bromide." When I first played this game, I was vaguely aware of "bromide" as a pharmacological term, so I figured this had to be some kind of super-secret potion. Nope. In Japanese, a *buromaido* refers to a printed photograph of a celebrity, named so for the silver bromide emulsions used in photography in the early twentieth century. Female bromides could often look a bit cheesecakey, like pin-up girls in magazine foldouts. When the party stumbles on this precious item, a crew of baddies burst into the room and attack. Why? Because we stole their spank material. Later on, we can trade this sexy photograph to a dirty old man for a power-up.

Females in *Chrono Trigger* are certainly more than just objects onto which sexual fantasies are projected, and the most egregious commodification of the female body only occurs within monster porn. While the game is often content to uphold traditional gender associations, it at least provides scenarios for women to be strong, capable characters, and not just quest objectives.

III

It's seven in the morning and I'm waiting in the chill of the station with a Mister Donut churro and a can of sweet hot coffee from the vending machine. There's only one morning bus to Moniwa Junior High, the furthest flung of all the schools in Fukushima, and it leaves at an ungodly 7:15 a.m.

Moniwa Junior High is a school of eleven students. Counting me, the staff outnumbers the student body. The entire second grade class is just one shy boy. Only about 500 people live in the small hamlet of Moniwa, a place famous primarily for its proximity to a dam and secondarily for its *onsen*—a public bath centered around a hot spring.

Everyone knows your business in Moniwa. And the things they don't know, they aren't exactly shy about finding out.

"*Maikeru-sensei, kekkon shiteimasu ka?*" the kids enjoy asking. "*Kanojo imasu ka?*" *Are you married? Do you have a girlfriend?* I answer with any number of deflections. Coming out in the workplace in Japan is not an idea I relish. I don't have the linguistic finesse to differentiate myself from the high-profile gay stereotypes on primetime TV, like Razor Ramon HG ("Hard Gay"), the heterosexual wrestler-comedian who dresses in skimpy leather and terrorizes unsuspecting senior citizens with eager thrusts of his pelvis. So I follow the advice of guys I've been dating, and keep my sex life and work life separated. "I'm far too handsome to be married yet!" I answer the children with faux-cocky American swagger.

One rainy autumn Saturday, my then-boyfriend and I and drive up the slick mountain roads to Moniwa. We have heard about their *onsen* and we have a hankering to bathe with strangers. The woman who waits with towels and locker keys at the reception area greets us both politely in Japanese, then speaks to me in hushed, fluent English. She's the mother of one of my students, and Filipina. She has been encouraging her daughter to speak English more at school, but the daughter is afraid of being singled out. *Of not being Japanese enough.*

We sit in the communal lounge, relaxed from the heat of the springs, rehydrating and waiting for the rain to let up. The student's mother shuffles over with a plate of pear slices and a pot of green tea. "For you and your friend," she says in English with a knowing smile, and then she retreats into the staff kitchen, back to the fog of heavy steam and thick Fukushima dialect.

•

Becoming the male heroes of adventure games and RPGs was never a huge shift in gender perspective for me. But I never *felt* the romances written for these protagonists.

They always seemed *artificial*. Great RPGs—and I consider many of Square's North American offerings during my youth to be great—not only engage us with entertaining gameplay but also captivate us emotionally. I felt a lot for these bright little collocations of pixels—their sadnesses, their triumphs, their struggles to overcome despair. But I couldn't sympathize with their drives for romantic love. Of course, I wasn't seeing anything in the game that looked like what I wanted. Not directly at least.

Achieving romantic love is rarely a goal in the type of games I've enjoyed. The first *Dragon Quest* features a save-the-damsel plotline, but like Mario's Peach and Link's Zelda, this princess is a mere MacGuffin—all three of them can be replaced with a mystic thingamabob or an ancient widget and the storylines would remain the same. Princesses are personified objects to be found and refurbished into lovers. Later games complicate romances by having them occur within the roster of PCs. But even female party members are not spared damselhood. Both *Final Fantasy IV*'s Rosa and *EarthBound*'s Paula need their male love interests—protagonists Cecil and Ness—to save them from captivity. And in *Chrono Trigger*, Crono must save his eventual bride and princess-in-disguise Marle from the prison of a dark dimension. And to do so, he first has to rescue her ancestor Queen Leene from her male captors.

Beyond continuing to treat women as earnable key items or kidnappable quest objectives, these narratives—no matter how subtly they integrate into the storyline—also privilege the idea of heterosexual love as *what romance is*. Now, there is absolutely nothing wrong with having a straight love story. But, it's often *the only story*—nonheterosexuality just isn't an option. As researcher Evan Lauteria notes, silent stand-ins like Crono who present the players with a feeling of control, also force an embedded sexuality onto the player. No matter what we envision for our blank avatar Crono, he's destined to be romantically linked to Marle. After the party's first catastrophic encounter with Magus, Crono is knocked out and has a dream—or vision?—of a spouselike Marle rousing him from sleep, much as Crono's mother does as the start of the game. Not only is Crono implied to be straight, then, but he's a little bit Oedipal too.

Unsurprisingly for a mass-market product of late 20th century Japan, *Chrono Trigger* demonstrates a clear bias toward heterosexuality. We can certainly categorize Crono and Marle as a straight couple. Meanwhile Robo's got his pink doppel-lover Atropos XR, and Ayla her willing sextoy Kino. But finding the places where sexuality isn't revealed is far more intriguing than cataloguing the game's sanctioned couples.

Lucca could be asexual—possibly even *robosexual*—though there is an alternate ending where we see Marle and Lucca ranking some of the NPCs as hot or not. Lucca goes so far as to call the knight Cyrus "a hunk" as her sprite flutters. Marle, preferring the scruffy charms of drunken treasure-hunter Toma, nevertheless speculates that he might have several girlfriends. In the DS version of this ending, Lucca rejoinders by wondering if he has *boyfriends*. They both giggle. Whatever Lucca's sexuality, she might be open to possibilities.

Frog, meanwhile, is even more of a puzzle. Unlike any of the other six party members, he has no known family members. His closest friend is hunky Cyrus, who protected him as a youth and for whom he squired faithfully. After Cyrus's death at the hands of Magus, Frog is haunted by his memory and seized by a desire to avenge him. After the girthy Masamune—broken when Cyrus fell—is long and firm again, Frog gets the thrust he needs to continue living. Later, the final exchange between Frog and Cyrus's ghost in the Northern Ruins is one of the gooiest, most melodramatic scenes in the game, but an interesting reward for having completed the tedious fetchquest and the sword-fighting foreplay with Cyrus's ghost that precedes it. As Cyrus's spirit fades into the beyond, Frog stammers, "Cyrus, wait! I … I…!" Neither of the North American versions nor the original Japanese offer a predicate to this delicate subject. Once again, however, an alternate ending adds a straight-up complication to the idea that Frog might be gay. In one ending, he is shown not only to have married Queen Leene, but also to have become the ancestor of Marle in the process.

But just as Marle and Lucca's male beauty pageant ending is difficult to resolve with Chrono canon—I know some of you will find a way!—we can also probably reject the implication that Marle might have werefrog DNA. And if it *is* a possible alternate timeline? Maybe Frog marries Leene out of his exaggerated sense of honor to Cyrus. Or maybe he's amphibisexual.

The architect of Glenn and Cyrus's parting, Magus, is similarly offbeat. Magus's attachment to his sister Schala is somewhere between the incestuous and the dutifully familial. It's difficult to envision a character as arrogant and power-hungry as Magus truly harboring romantic affection. The almost impossible task of finding Schala again is an adequate way to occupy this megalomaniac. If anything turns Magus on, it's *power*.

And he's not the only one aroused by power. Although a minor character and a boss as annoying as his bloodsucking namesake, Magus's general Flea is the most overt representation of alternate sexual identity in *Chrono Trigger*. Although Flea looks female, he identifies as male. Nevertheless, Flea is keenly aware of his ambiguous sexuality and his queer anthem is potent—"Male or female, what difference does it make? Power is beautiful, and I've got the power."

As a boss, Flea flits about the battle screen dramatically under his billowing cape, stopping sometimes to laugh exaggeratedly, to strike a pose, or to emit a little pink anime heart. Besides voguing, Flea uses hands-off status-affecting attacks—one blows a kiss. Much as his alternate take on gender roles baffles the party, Flea can literally confuse our characters during battle, causing them to attack each other. Just as with a few of Ayla's techs, heart symbols are embedded in some of Flea's attack names.[7] And if Ayla uses her Charm ability on Flea later on in the game, she can steal the Flea Vest, an item more accurately translated in the DS version as the "Flea Bustier." Yup, he's wearing a bra. And if you find this item in *Chrono Cross*, only male characters can equip it.

BradyGames's strategy guide for *Chrono Trigger* insists on appending a half-assed interrobang each and *every* time the masculine pronoun is used in reference to Flea: "[H]it him(!?) with your best magic and away he(!?) goes." On the Japanese side, the guide *Chrono Trigger: the Complete* warns the reader: "You must not be fooled by appearances. It's actually a man!"[8] The more recent Japanese guide *Chrono Trigger: Ultimania* describes Flea as "on first sight a beautiful female human, but is a

---

7   Like "The Stare ♡ / Flea's ♡♡Magic."
8   "姿にだまされてはいけない。実は男なんだ！"

respected Mystic man."[9] In the Japanese version of the game, Flea uses the personal pronoun *atai*, a colloquial feminine pronoun that strongly contrasts with Frog's rough masculine pronoun *ore*—in Japanese, by the way, there are at least a dozen ways to say "I," depending on one's gender, age, situation, or preference. *Atai* is not an everyday pronoun either. It is a variant of the pronoun *atashi*, a term I often heard used performatively by gay men. While Flea may be a man playing at womanhood, he is not exactly an authentic representation of transgender identity or even of drag performance.

Flea might be much better described as an *okama*, but even this term is fraught. *Okama* is not always a derogatory word for gay men, but it's not flattering either. It's innocuous enough, however, to appear in strategy guide *Chrono Trigger: the Perfect*—who names these things, anyway?—which tells the player that Flea will "berate you using *okama* language."[10] Well, that's pretty direct. *Okama* can mean anything from a careless synonym for "gay," to a man in women's clothing exhibiting stereotypically effeminate mannerisms. Often these two concepts are conflated, and as sociologist James Valentine puts it, "[i]n media portrayals okama look like fakes, trying to be women but noticeably

---

9 "見た目は美しい人間の女性だが、れっきとした魔族の男。"
10 "オカマ言葉で激しくなじる。"

failing." Indeed, that spectacular failure might explain why these *okama* characters are often featured on comedy shows on Japanese television. Flea, on the other hand, succeeds extremely well at "passing" for female.

While Flea is largely an inconsequential character, his attack strategy reflects some real-world truths about nontraditional genderings. Some people turn a blind eye to them, while others become confused and enraged. The biggest threat to our well-being doesn't come from people like Flea, but rather from *our reactions* to them.

•

The fantasy world of *Chrono Trigger* is a foreign country, with different demography and cultural norms. Just as it's unfair for me to extend my American expectations to my stay in Japan, it's also unwise to judge a fictional realm by the same standards as we'd judge our own. Or to expect that world to look like ours. In fact, it is the very difference between fictional worlds and our own that make us want to enter them.

At the same time, fantasy realms are both derivatives and disguised versions of our own world—at least, pockets of that world. So far we've only taken a look at the inhabitants of this alternate reality. But larger institutions surround the cast and characters of *Chrono Trigger*, some so subtly integrated into gameplay that we may encounter them without even noticing.

STEEL AND PURE LOGIC

THE WORLD OF TOMORROW OF yesterday has not yet come.

The 1950s sci-fi dream of domed cities, meals in a pill, and helper "robits" has fizzled into failed Biosphere experiments, Clif Bars, and Roombas. And the Epcot-esque monorails and treadmill sidewalks? Merely secondary transports to and from gigantic fuel-guzzling airplanes. Just where is the future we were promised?

The future of *Chrono Trigger* is a bleak industrial landscape of shattered cities and lawless ruins. Humans huddle in fear while monsters roam unchecked. Life has been distorted, stunted, and starved. This is the kind of future we were warned about by the Orwells and Atwoods, the Huxleys and Zamyatins. But their futures, no matter how dystopian, were still full of *people*. People simply behaving as people always have—oppressing, dominating, lying, controlling, self-deceiving.

Chrono Trigger's 2300 AD is a future where people have become irrelevant. The world has moved on, and humans have been left in its dust. Those who survive live in terror of mutated monstrosities and killbot patrols. Is this completely the fault of Lavos, breaking free from the core of the planet and scorching the globe with hellfire? Or did humans play a part in their own demise?

We have very little information on 1999 AD, except for a brief visual record of Lavos's emergence. There isn't even a complete world map for this era—just the cutout of a future that never came to be. Superhighways and domed communities have replaced the towns and castles of 999 years ago, the "present." But the lush greenery of 1000 AD has become less verdant. Deserts surround the Truce Dome where Crono's hometown once was, and to the east, the guru Melchior's hut has long been swallowed up by the sands.

Building the world of tomorrow has its costs, and humanity has taken out a huge loan from the planet. But 1999 AD is the year the planet is about to go bankrupt. The reappearance of Lavos after scores of millions of years is a convenient, but ultimately simplistic answer to a question we must ask:

Just what was the year 2000 AD shaping up to be?

•

1999 AD. Our world. Plans for the new millennium are ramping up. Party animals arrange for lavish New Year's Eve celebrations, reserving halls, caterers, and performers. They will ring in the new year in opulence, one-upping their social rivals' celebratory shindigs. Doomsday preppers stockpile for New Year's Day, collecting clean water, canned food, and fuel for their generators. They will survive the new year in comfort, and shut out the ill-prepared and foolish. Y2K is coming.

The Y2K bug was a widely fearmongered computer glitch supposed to have calamitous effects on modern civilization, and all because lazy programmers had been recording years in two digits instead of four. So when the year 1999 (stored as the abbreviated "99") rolled into 2000 ("00"), computers would think it was 1900 all over again. As we have all learned from science fiction, logic errors are a leading cause of spectacular machine failure—trailing just behind laser cannons and perplexing human emotions. And it was these emotionally confused, laser-toting logic-broken machines that would fire all of their ammunition into humanity when the clock struck midnight on January 1, 2000.

•

We begin our tale in *Chrono Trigger* in Guardia, 1000 AD—*the present*. This present is rustic. Nostalgic. Technology is not unknown, but its applications are largely the stuff of turn-of-the-twentieth-century world's fairs. *Ride the intercity ferry that runs on* steam*, only 10G a trip! See the marvelous battling-singing automaton! Knock him down and win a prize!* Technology may be mischievous, but it's not yet dangerous—unless a spring-loaded boxing-glove in the solar plexus knocks your HP to zero. The anxieties of 999 AD have been forgotten with the celebratory Millennial Fair, commemorating 1000 years of unbroken monarchy. Despite a significant amount of armed personnel, Guardia lacks any noticeable military-industrial complex to support its boots on the ground. In fact, besides the Truce-Porre ferry, the only revolutionary technological advances are those contributed by our resident science geek Lucca.

Well, most of them. The modern Chancellor of Guardia—probably the insectoid monster boss Yakra XIII in disguise—has the powerful Dragon Tank under his control. The three-part boss isn't too tough a customer. Unlike other bosses, it doesn't taunt the party with in-battle dialogue. It attacks, counterattacks, and heals, all according to its programming. "Machines aren't capable of evil," Lucca sighs as she fixes the broken-down Robo, "Humans make them that way." If we believe Lucca, we have a big ontological problem with Robo being a willing helper of our party. Is Lucca reprogramming Robo, or merely resetting him to factory defaults? An inquiry into Robo's autonomy prompts a larger question about 2300 AD's inhabitants.

In the depths of the machine-automated Geno Dome, the supercomputer Mother Brain calculates the end of humanity and the rise of the machines. "Don't you understand?" she questions the party over the Dome's speakers. "This planet would be peaceful if there were no humans around." Humans are an unwanted variable in her equation of existence, but a necessary factor in her genesis. Long before Mother Brain was an antagonistic presence to humans, was she the artificial intelligence that kept this Dome running? We know nothing about the history of the Geno Dome, and whether it was founded by humans or the monsters in Medina, who beseech their legendary god-king: "Oh, great Magus, why didn't you simply exterminate the human race 400 years ago?"

In all likelihood, it was not monsters but humans who created the technology that would outgrow them, threaten them, and eventually seek to eliminate them completely. In a world without Asimov's Laws of Robotics, Mother Brain operates only on the flawed subroutines established by her programmers. Although her goals are antithetical to our party's, Mother Brain is also a success story. She has built the closest thing the future has to a government. "We robots will create a new order," she prophesies over the loudspeakers. "A nation of steel, and pure logic. A true paradise!"

•

1000 AD is the closest any era in *Chrono Trigger* comes to paradisiacal. Monsters pose little menace to humankind—indeed, some even live in human towns. There are no interspecies wars, no genocidal dictators. People seem content in the Kingdom of Guardia.

The Guardia castle is a dominating structure, the largest architectural element in the world. The town of Truce where we begin the story is surely under the authority of Guardia and recognizes it as sovereign. Porre to the south and Choras directly west of Porre also recognize the monarchy. The map design also aesthetically links the commonwealth with blue roofs. The independent city-state of Medina where most civilized monsters dwell is firmly a red state.

The Guardian government seems to unite most of the globe, and probably has since at least 600 AD when maroon roofing was all the rage. In both eras, the government operates as a federal monarchy. Each town is governed by a mayor, who tends to live in the largest house. Whether these positions are hereditary or electoral is not clear, but it appears that mayoral privileges tend to stay within the family. When our party seeks the stolen Sun Stone in an endgame sidequest, the trick to taking it from the covetous mayor of Porre in 1000 AD is to bribe an ancestor of his living in the mayor's house in 600 AD with a gift—hey, I wouldn't turn down free jerky either. Returning back to 1000 AD, we find the Porre mayor a changed man, now beloved by his family, having been inculcated with a generations-long valuing of charity. Meanwhile, in the monster-run Medina, Ozzie VIII relies on his ancestor's fame to rule the town according to his whims. If the position of mayor is not inherited, then the voters of *Chrono Trigger* love a good dynasty.

As one might expect from a game that employs time travel as a major plot device, dynasticism plays a large role in our story. Several other characters are conveniently roman-numeraled descendants of major players. Toma XIII and Yakra XIII continue their forebears' legacies of treasure-hunting and chancellor-impersonating, respectively. Banta the blacksmith in 600 AD who yearns for an intelligent daughter is most likely the ancestor of the anagrammatic Taban, father of Lucca. Woodworking and alcoholism run in the family of the Choras carpenter. And of course, the bloodline of Guardia runs all the way from 65,000,000 BC to 2300 AD, from prehistoricouple Ayla and Kino to an old man in 2300 AD. Of this unbroken line, however, we have clear record of only two actual monarchs—Kings Guardia XXI and XXXIII.

As expected, both the 21st and 33rd rulers are male—and it seems their wives have married into the family. Queen Leene, for whom Marle is mistaken, is not a direct member of the Guardia line. "The Queen married into the family 10 years ago," gossips a young woman in Guardia palace in 600 AD. And even though Leene has a seat in the throne room, a villager in 600 AD Truce tells us, "It's the year 600, and the 21st King of Guardia reigns." As we learn from the example of Queen Zeal, in the world of *Chrono Trigger*, the monarchs seem to inherit the name of their kingdoms as their personal names upon enthronement. We can therefore guess that Aliza, mother of Marle, is also an intermarrier. But lacking any other rulers for comparison, it is unclear how rulership is passed down through successive generations. We are then left to wonder who will inherit the throne after Guardia XXXIII dies or abdicates. Marle, who is really Princess Nadia, is a likely successor. At least until she marries Crono, which is not only the fairy-tale subtext of their romantic subplot, but also the ending suggested by the final FMV.

So, who is the next leader of Guardia? Will it be Queen Guardia XXXIV, or perhaps King Crono the Silent? Neither *Chrono Trigger* nor its sequels provide the answer to this question of monarchical legacy. Although gender roles tend to skew patriarchal, the crown should rightfully fall to Marle.

After all, it wouldn't be fit to have a king with a criminal past.

•

Crono's trial is one of the most theatrical scenes in early Square history. The Dream Team, the three major producers of *Chrono Trigger*, wanted to craft a scenario that would echo the famous opera sequence from *Final Fantasy VI*, and Crono's trial is indeed cinematic. Panning down into forced perspective of the courtroom, we are treated with a new piece of playful but tense theme music. The stained glass backdrop of the room depicts Justice not as a blind woman, but rather as an old man holding a balance adorned with flowers. And why shouldn't justice be old and male? The jury who will decide Crono's guilt or innocence in Marle's kidnapping are all identical elderly men.

The trial serves as a brief reminder of one of the most hallowed tenets of time travel—what you do in the past affects your future. Except now we don't have the luxury of reliving the events of the Millennial Fair and choosing to become the model fairgoer. Did we accidentally eat that packed lunch sitting unattended? Strike against us. Did we not help that little girl find her cat? Strike. While food theft might be considered indicative of deep-seated evil, a lack of samaritanism is just plain unfair. No one else at the fair helped this girl find her goddamn cat, but suddenly Crono is to blame? This trial is a sham. With paltry evidence of any real wrongdoing and a desire for mischief, the prosecuting Chancellor attempts to assassinate Crono's character in the hopes of eventually assassinating the rest of him.

We're not alone in this. Since Crono doesn't have much of a voice, Pierre the lawyer will speak for us. Pierre's sprite is the same one that appears as a merchant in many towns. He might be a bit of a shyster—"Whew… Looks like they're buying it," he nudges Crono mid-trial—but he's on our side and we get him *pro bono*. As witnesses come forward to testify for or against Crono, we have the option of giving binary answers to the Chancellor's probing and tricky questions. "Who actually started this whole mess?" he grills Crono. We can choose one of two equally damning replies. "I did" seems to be an admission of guilt, while "Marle did" seems to be an affront to the royal family. Peppering his accusations with loaded words like "terrorist," the Chancellor sure knows how to rouse the rabble.

When both prosecution and defense rest, the jury members hobble into the center of the courtroom. Their verdict need not be unanimous, but the careless player can easily get seven votes for guilty. As the votes are tallied, the jurors move to the right for innocent, and to left for guilty. Sorry, southpaws. The spectators' reactions to these votes are ambiguous—Super Nintendo cartridges rarely produced faithful human vocalizations—but each "guilty" seems to illicit a whistling, cheering sound, and each "not guilty" a grumbling boo. This crowd is out for blood.

And blood they just might get, because if Crono is found guilty, the judge will sentence him to death after a three-day period of solitary confinement. Even if the jury finds Crono unanimously not guilty, he's still *not innocent*. The judge will sentence Crono to three days of solitary anyway, simply for having run off with Marle. And if the judge rules in our favor, the Chancellor will ignore the law and schedule Crono for execution. "The paperwork's probably just been held up in the system!" he insists to the warden.

One of the gravest warnings I had received before I went to Japan was *don't get arrested*. I intended not to. But I felt at times dangerously close to people who might be criminals. Rumors circulated that proprietors of a local punk bar I frequented were arrested for marijuana possession when their business abruptly shut down. Weed is as criminalized as heroin in Japan. And I knew of some people, both native Japanese and expats, who enjoyed a smoke now and then. I was scared shitless of being hauled in for questioning, so I steered clear.

Just as in Guardia, in Japan the burden of proof is on you, not the state. Blogger Eric Yosomono paints a terrible picture of being arrested in Japan—of brutal interrogations, of a system designed at all levels to convict you, of depressing and demeaning prison conditions. We can explore the Guardia jail at length during Crono's breakout, finding awful instruments of torture and even a prisoner left waiting in a guillotine. This young man, Fritz, later explains that he was arrested without trial. But surely he must have done something wrong. "After all," Yosomono writes of his experience, "how could anyone ever get arrested unless they were guilty, right?"

As Crono is taken away to the tower for imprisonment, the King restrains Marle. "Even royalty must obey rules," he reminds his distraught daughter, both blaming her for the events that led to this ugly episode as well as washing his hands of the entire affair.

His words will come back to haunt him. When the party recovers the mythical and gargantuan Rainbow Shell in 600 AD, they leave the treasure at Guardia Castle for safekeeping. Flashing forward to the present, the shell—rather, its disappearance—has suddenly become the central piece of evidence in "the trial of the century." While the text at this point in the game gets a little slapdash, we learn that King Guardia XXXIII himself has been accused of not only stealing the priceless heirloom, but also pawning it for cash. Our mystery-solving party is on the case. After retrieving evidence of the shell's existence in the castle's treasury, the party bursts into the courtroom through the stained glass window to exonerate the king and to unmask the false Chancellor as Yakra XIII, who has created havoc to avenge his ancestor's death.

Exposing Yakra XIII's fraud should allow us to clear any misconceptions we had held about the Guardian legal system and its chancery for convicting innocents like Fritz, Crono, and finally the king himself. The system was fine, right? It was just corruption that caused it to malfunction so lethally. But in an ironic conclusion, the instigator of all of this mischief, Yakra XIII, gets no trial—he is executed on the spot by the party. Whether guillotine or katana, there is little argument against the cold logic of steel.

•

Or gold, for that matter.

As in most traditional RPGs, gold is an enormously useful commodity in *Chrono Trigger*—one that has value across all cultures and eras, whether or not it is immediately recognized as money. Even monsters recognize the utility of carrying cash. Beating them up and taking their gold like a bunch of well-armed schoolyard bullies is apparently the highest earning occupation out there.

Second only to this as a money-making enterprise is the mercantile industry, present in all time periods.

Of course, merchants must acquire their goods from somewhere. People need to brew tonics, construct shelters, forge iron swords, and sew leather cuirasses. Not to mention those specialty items! If seasoned warriors Crono and Marle can't equip firearms, then we certainly can't expect most common folk to wield them. And how many robots out there need new battle-limbs? Supply and demand must mean nothing to the economy, since few people seem to be armed with weapons while the shops stock infinite numbers of them. More confusingly, items grow ever more luxurious and expensive as our party journeys onward. While this falls firmly in step with sound game mechanics, it also throws the concept of technological progress out the window. Shops in 600 AD sell much better equipment than some present day places, and even the great sage Melchior's Masamune, forged from a substance so precious it hasn't been seen for eons, is much less powerful than the Flash Blade we can purchase from a ragged survivor in 12,000 BC. A man so poor that even the tidy sum of 18,000G won't help his family advance in the world.

Meanwhile, inflation simply does not exist in the timeline of *Chrono Trigger*. The price of tonic remains 10G from 65,000,000 BC all the way to 2300 AD. And neither of these eras understands what "G" means as a currency. In prehistory, most meaningful trade is accomplished through bartering objects like feathers and flower petals, and you'll even get a few freebies like the healing "sweet water." Our party can nevertheless purchase basic items like tonics for gold, or as the cavefolk call it, "shiny stone." Far in the future, tonics are still available. The merchants dubiously accept gold as cash—"You call this money?"—but one wonders what type of economy the post-apocalypse can support. While the merchants may have been the lowest social class in pre-modern Japan—ranking fourth below samurai, farmers, and craftsmen—they are the most visible evidence of economic activity throughout the ages.

Other professions of course support our narrative and gameplay. Innkeepers provide spaces to heal our party, and the greater hospitality industry employs many other barkeeps and servers to run the pubs, where some of the juiciest, quest-advancingest gossip circulates. The growing transportation industry between Truce and Porre hints at a new kind of industry. Careers in the military are a popular choice in the latter half of the first millennium AD—there are at least 39 knights and soldiers in 600 AD, when Guardia faced Magus's forces, and 22 active military personnel in Guardia even in the peaceful 1000 AD. And while many of these occupations, especially the military, tend to attract men, there are still career paths for women. Even in the clergy.

•

For a country with such a conspicuously large building for worship, there is little religion in Guardia. Once we've defeated the four false nuns in the cathedral in 600 AD, there are few visible people actively engaged in religious life, and most of them are women of the cloth. So why this massive Christian-like cathedral, which surely cost enough G to make even the gougiest merchant retire from sales?

The answer lies in that non-canonical ending where Frog and Queen Leene tie the knot in 600 AD. As the credits roll, the duo advances up the aisle. A man dressed in Zealish garb waits behind the altar to officiate the ceremony. While the back end of the cathedral may be a secret refuge for Guardia royalty, or perhaps the quarters of the priests and nuns, the chapel at the front is purely for ceremony. It is likely that the funeral of Guardia XXI was held here, since in this alternate ending Leene is free to marry again. Unless polywog polygamy is totally cool in medieval Guardia.

Back in our world, and many miles west from the center of Fukushima City, lies St. Anna's Garden, a picturesque tourism spot that features the Michinoku microbrewery, an ice cream shop, and ample opportunities for antiquing. At the entrance to this little shopping village where I spent several totally heterosexual man-dates is a single-aisled chapel adorned with stained glass windows. Unlike the vaguely Christian image of the winged figure in *Chrono Trigger*'s cathedral, St. Anna's Church displays a triptych of Jesus crucified, resurrected, and returned to his disciples. Most who visit St. Anna's Church, however, do not pray to Anna, mother of the Virgin Mary, or to Christ himself. With roughly only 1% of Japanese professing Christianity, St. Anna's Church doesn't even offer regular church services. But it does perform weddings galore.

Historically, the most popular form of wedding in Japan was Shintō, which as the state religion of Japan naturally monopolized the marriage industry. Even up to the 1980s, Shintō-style weddings accounted for more than 90% of all ceremonies. I had the chance to attend a Shintō wedding in 2005, and it was almost unintelligible to me. Then again, it was conducted in archaic Japanese, and I was drunk on ritual sake.

This wedding was an anomaly for two major reasons. First, the groom was a white foreigner and the bride a Japanese resident of Fukushima, neither of whom could understand the ceremonial language much either. Second, by 2005 the Christian-style wedding had long been the choice for marrying couples, though like all imports it would be given some uniquely Japanese flavors. As social anthropologist Michael Fisch notes, the officiants of Christian-style weddings in Japan don't even need to be ordained ministers. They can simply be hired actors—especially white males—who look and dress the part. Fisch, a self-described Jew and dual Israeli-American citizen, even worked as a hired priest to study the phenomenon of Christian-style weddings.

So in this alternate ending sometime after our party first visits 600 AD, a priest or perhaps an actor bedecked in a traditional costume—close to thirteen millennia out of fashion by this point—celebrates the marriage of Frog and Leene in a church vaguely dedicated to some sort of angelic being. The only known visitor to cathedral is the 600 AD Chancellor, who is of course Yakra in disguise. Perhaps the association of organized religion with monsters was prevalent enough for citizens to abandon the cathedral. By 1000 AD the building has vanished from the map, having been swallowed by the Guardia Forest.

Our journey into the cathedral in 600 AD finds us face to face with an idol of Magus, whom the monsters worship as a god on earth. Four hundred years later in Medina village, this statue has survived, and adherents still sing songs to their fiendlord. After our party defeats Magus in 600 AD and he is hurled backward through time to his home era, the leadership of monsterdom has been usurped by his henchchief Ozzie. The Medinans no longer offer praise to the statue of Magus, but rather to the graven image of Ozzie himself. After we trounce Ozzie in 600 AD for the final time, this second statue vanishes, leaving nothing but an unadorned agora.

By removing these false gods one after the other, we complete the process of civilizing the savage monsters by dismantling their entire belief system. Way to go, light-skinned Guardia imperialists!

The elimination of organized religion, however, is not the full subtext of our sidequests. In the ideal, all-quests-cleared timeline of *Chrono Trigger*, religion—or at least the *idea* of religion—still has its place. When the party completes the quest to make Fiona's Forest grow, the former site of conservationist Fiona's home in 600 AD has been replaced with a shrine. Inside, nuns offer prayers to the once again broken-down body of Robo, whom we instruct to help reforest the land for several centuries before the party zips casually to the present in their time machine to find him completely lifeless. After rescuing and repairing Robo for the third time, the shrine is left without its relic. Upon our return, we can see that the primary object of veneration has become a seed, a symbol which holds significance for people of many eras. Whether Fiona's Shrine is a religious place or a sparse museum is up for debate. The nun who shamelessly hawks her wares inside the shrine suggests that like St. Anna, fertile Fiona has become a patron saint of thinly-disguised commerce.

•

Y2K came and went without global destruction in its wake. The stone juggernaut of the Mayan calendar completed its full turn in 2012, and we were not crushed under the wheel of the new b'ak'tun. We survived. The Earth survived. And it hasn't stopped moving.

This world moves fast, but we do not feel the motions of our planet, rotating on its axis, wobbling its way around the Sun. We observe them only through the passing of day into night, from season begetting new season. The world moves slow, and we do not experience the subtle drifts of continents, the creation of new land masses from the old. We guess these changes only through fossil records and jigsaw cartography.

Our view into the planet upon which the action of *Chrono Trigger* largely takes place gives us the exact opposite of the information that we are used to. We see little in the way of days becoming nights. Our trips through time, however, show a world heavily active with plate tectonics and shifting geography. The Pangaea-like globe of 65,000,000 BC is unrecognizable from the archipelago of 2300 AD. Even between 600 and 1000 AD, the three central islands have reconfigured into one large landmass. This world has seen its fair share of global changes at frightening, illogical speeds.

What has led to these huge geographical shifts? If we believe the majority of roman numerals appended to names, such drastic changes can occur over only twelve human generations. This is a world in flux, and not just from the effects of time travelers. The constant shifts of the lithosphere must accompany any number of earthquakes and ruptures, leaving people to wonder when The Big One is coming, and what destruction it might bring.

They will get their answer in 1999 AD.

THE DAY OF LAVOS

MARCH 11, 2011 AD. THE strongest earthquake ever to hit Japan struck just off the coast of the city of Sendai, causing widespread damage and fires. The quake triggered a massive tsunami that desolated the northeast coastline of Honshū as it spread throughout the Pacific Ocean to places as far away as Chile. Pounding the shores of Japan at heights of up to twenty feet, this surge of water washed away entire towns, drowning and sweeping away thousands of residents. The tidal wave breached the walls of the Fukushima Daiichi Nuclear Power Plant roughly 60 miles down the coast from Sendai, causing a meltdown that directly irradiated the environment within 50 miles of the facility. Strong winds carried fallout even further inland. With the toll of dead and missing estimated to be as high as 20,000, and with radioactive material still actively seeping into the Pacific Ocean as of this writing, the Great East Japan Earthquake stands as one of worst disasters in Japanese history.

Meanwhile, exactly sixteen years before this national crisis, gamers across Japan were beginning their simultaneous journeys through time to stop another disaster from annihilating humankind and reshaping the world into a wasteland. *Chrono Trigger* made its shelf debut on March 11, 1995 in Japan, just nine days before the Aum Shinrikyō cult released sarin gas—a powerful nerve agent—on the Tokyo subway system, killing thirteen and sickening countless others.

Shōkō Asahara, Aum's founder and leader, had styled himself as a new Jesus Christ. Borrowing heavily from the Bible, Asahara predicted that the forces of evil—in the guise of the United States—would initiate World War III. This war would end in nothing less than global nuclear armageddon. Only the chosen would survive.

While the exact reasons for the attacks have never fully come to light, I can imagine Asahara, Magus-like, tampering with forces of destruction beyond his control. Before he was Shōkō Asahara he was Chizuo Matsumoto, a poor boy in a working class family. Completely blind in one eye and only partially sighted in the other, this seventh of nine children may have understood exactly what it feels like to be stepped on. And just like Janus—the vulnerable boy Magus had been before being displaced in time—Chizuo grew up to be a prophet, and he prophesied the end of the world. As his cult grew, its bizarre propaganda drifted further into public view. The warning signs were there, and they were not heeded.

With a few foreshocks rumbling days before it happened, the Great East Japan Earthquake did not come without forewarning either. But it was unexpected nonetheless. And in another world, in another reality, the Day of Lavos erupts with earth-shattering fury, ushering in a waking nightmare for all humankind.

•

65,000,000 BC. Crono, Ayla and their third companion defeat Azala in her fortress. The reptites seemed far more likely to inherit the earth than what Azala derisively calls "the apes." Only through the coincidental arrival of Crono's crew are these cavepeople able to defeat their technologically superior reptilian foes.

Well, if not coincidence then synchronicity. Because it is in just this unlikely evenly-divisible year that Lavos is about to make its unwelcome and cataclysmic appearance on the planet.

As Azala crawls forward from the afterimage of her fearsome steed—there will be no Black Tyrano in the fossil record—the tense theme "Boss Battle 1" fades to silence. Then, the plaintive "At the Bottom of the Night" underscores Ayla's respect and sympathy for her worthy rival Azala. But rather than function as a melodramatic backdrop for what should surely be Azala's repentance, this sentimental tune becomes the eerie soundtrack to Lavos's crash-landing. Through a stream of cold distant lights the "red star" hurtles through space, growing thornier and ever more menacing, following a parabola towards the earth as a synthesized symphony resigns the world to impending doom.

As it approaches, Ayla christens the unholy meteoroid "Lavos"—in her apparently postpositive-adjectival language, *la* means "fire," and *vos* "big." This is not a detail created for North American localization. Present in the Japanese version as *Ravosu*, the name had in my adult walkthrough of the game suggested a nod to *Ravukurafuto*, the Japanese rendering of horror author H.P. Lovecraft.

•

After the guru Melchior is freed from the Mountain of Woe in 12,000 BC, he tells the party that "Lavos sleeps deep underground, while consuming the energy of this planet." This phrase reminded me of the well-known Lovecraft line, "In his house at R'lyeh, dead Cthulhu waits dreaming."

Lavos is, like many of the more powerful denizens of Lovecraftian lore, an ancient being from beyond the known universe. Its powers are immense, its purpose sinister and fearsomely logical—the utter ruin of the world for its own gain. Lavos is given a godlike status by Queen Zeal, who, like many unfortunate Lovecraft characters, is driven mad by its sheer power.

Lavos, however, is not an inconceivable, amorphous horror like many of Lovecraft's creations. The gargantuan space hedgehog that slams into the world of *Chrono Trigger* is deadly physical and highly resilient. It survives and causes several global catastrophes, one of which leads to an ice age. It is barely perturbed by the rise and fall of the Kingdom of Zeal, arrogantly torn free of the bounds of gravity by magic to hover Laputa-like over a world of muggles, only to crash humiliated into the earth again. Hidden deep in the core of the planet, disturbed only occasionally by the insistence of misguided summoners like Queen Zeal and her temporally displaced son, Lavos bides its time.

When Lavos arrives, it is not heralded by madmen or fanatics. The Prophet of Zeal—Janus-turned-Magus in disguise—has no dire warnings for the people of 1999 AD. Thought to exist only in creation myths perhaps, Lavos bursts out of the planet in a shower of undeniably real fire and terror. To the everyday people of *Chrono Trigger*, what emerges is a *kaijū*, a giant monster. An erinaceous Godzilla with none of the endearing qualities.

•

Before he was a massive proto-pokémon protecting Japan against mecha versions of himself, or teaming up with his bumbling nephew Godzooky to solve mysteries in small-screen Hanna-Barbera animation, Godzilla was a fearsome monster, a tortured product of atomic experimentation gone wrong.

The film *Gojira* was released in Japan in 1954, nine years after the United States dropped two atomic bombs on Hiroshima and Nagasaki. Little Boy and Fat Man, two blunt American-style *kaijū*, were the worst weapons the world had seen and the ugliest harbingers of the atomic age. Gojira—or as we better know him, Godzilla—began as an embodiment of Japanese nuclear rage, of a people punished brutally for the sins of its leadership. Both aggressor and victim, Godzilla rampages through Tokyo until he is defeated by a weapon even deadlier than the one that mutated him. The film ends with the lingering fear of creating an even worse monster.

Lavos too is a spiny-backed creature of flame that destroys indiscriminately. But unlike Godzilla, it is not a victim of human interference. When Queen Zeal attempts to harness its abilities for her selfish gain, Lavos is already a being of immense power, having had precisely 64,988,000 years to leech energy from the planet.

But, is Lavos actually *evil*? Most of the villains in the Square pantheon are insatiable megalomaniacs, and many of them harbor a sociopathic hatred of life itself.

Chrono Trigger's answer to *Final Fantasy IV*'s Zemus, or to *FF6*'s Kefka, is Queen Zeal. She, like these other fiends, channels her lust for power and disdain for weakness into a final form. Shedding their humanoid appearances, these villains achieve monstrous apotheoses, becoming beautiful, surrealistic abominations. But Queen Zeal is not our final foe. *We don't even have to fight her*. It is Lavos who beckons.

After we break into the outer shell of Lavos, we follow throbbing biorhythms to what seems like its core. There, a grotesquely large biomechanoid crowds the screen. Our party comes to understand that Lavos "has slept underground, controlling evolution on this world for his own purpose," and that eventually Lavos's spawn "must migrate to other planets… to repeat the cycle."

Unlike the cast of *Chrono Trigger*, I have real difficulty imagining Lavos as male. Lavos is too big, too inhuman, too godlike to be anthropomorphized as a "him." Regardless of the party's gendering of their enemy, if their collective hypothesis is indeed true, then humankind actually owes its existence to Lavos. Even ignoring the convenient fact that Lavos's appearance saved humanity from extinction at the hands of the reptites, if Lavos *did* shape all of life for its own gain, we cannot remove it from the equation. There's a reason we can't stop Lavos from ever appearing on our planet. *We would not exist without it.*

Battling through Lavos's second transformation, we finally see its final form, a triptych boss comprising an oversized biped flanked by two floating pods. Lavos's evolution occurs in reverse in comparison with the regular Square baddies, shrinking from monster-sized to near-humanoid in a twisted *apanthroposis*. Humans were Lavos's pet project, and it has refashioned itself in their image.

Is Lavos a selfish conqueror of the world, or a planetary farmer simply following its instincts? How sentient is Lavos, and if it can speak to us, why won't it? Do apiarists palaver with their bees, or do they just mind the hives and collect the honey? It's painful to imagine our species as *insects*, as fodder for something bigger, more powerful. Something that could plummet from above and ruin us in the blink of an eye.

·

1974 AD. Nippon Hōsō Kyōkai, Japan's public broadcasting corporation, held a campaign soliciting artwork from Japanese citizens to memorialize the atomic bombings from nearly 30 years prior. Of the 975 pieces collected and exhibited in Hiroshima in August of that year, 101 were chosen for publication.

Unforgettable Fire is as beautiful as it is terrifying. If the postscript to the book is to be believed, none of the contributing artists were professionals. Indeed, many of the drawings are rough, primitivist, dominated by grays and reds. Dismembered, disfigured, and destitute characters float through limbo-like landscapes. For all of these artists, the memory of Little Boy's leveling of Hiroshima is vivid, whether they were well into their 80s or as young as their 30s.

The work of one then-36-year-old artist captured my attention immediately. Tsutomu Ojiri remembers having seen the A-bomb falling from the sky. A five panel time-lapse begins with one large red circle and a smaller red circle underneath. Going right to left—Japanese style—the top ball seems to shrink as the lower one grows larger and larger, extending from a crude red lightning bolt. The fireball gradually dwarfs the sun until it is monstrous and starlike itself, too big to fit in the final panel. I couldn't help but imagine Tsutomu as young boy, seeing that horrible Lavosian red fireball barreling towards him.

Other images in this catalog are less vivid but equally evocative. Yūji Ichida—age 64 at time of drawing—depicts a despairing woman, fully clothed, holding a small naked form in her hands. Behind her, a dead animal. And behind that, ruin. Piles of debris, trees stripped of all leaves and standing haunted in a hazy waste. If this is the aftermath of apocalypse, then we are lucky not to travel through the broken world of 1999 AD after Lavos arises volcanic from his slumber.

I last saw Fukushima City in the summer of 2009, three years after I had moved back from Japan to the U.S. On the surface, nothing much had changed in my absence. But my old haunts felt more like ghost towns. Quieter. Emptier. I knew almost nobody, and nobody knew me. Whatever magic there had been had largely dissipated. I felt out of place. Out of time.

Two years later, when the combined forces of nature and man—*magic* and *tech*?—collided to form a triple disaster on March 11, I was frantic. I texted, sent hasty emails. All of them the same: "*Daijōbu?*" *Are you OK?* Friends in the Tokyo area and the Tōhoku Region alike responded. *Yes, we're OK, but…*

There's always a *but*. Japanese is a language of ambiguities, a language of un-finishing each other's sentences. But these *but*s continued into grim new clauses. *But my friend's grandmother was swept away by the tsunami. But our home is wrecked and we are sheltering at the elementary school. But we are afraid to go outside because of the radiation.*

Several months later, an ex-boyfriend living in Tokyo—but a Fukushiman by birth—told me about what was going on in the city where I once lived a comfortable expatriate life. His family's dogs couldn't go out for walks because of the radiation. Worse, the local children weren't allowed out to play. Even worse, fewer local children remained in Fukushima—many families had fled the city in panic.

I remembered long bicycle rides along the Abukuma River, treks up Hanamiyama to see the view of Mount Shinobu protruding nipple-like from the center of the city. I remembered my students—middle-schoolers in their sailor uniforms, elementary-schoolers shouldering carapaccan *randoseru* bookbags. I remembered the wizened, overtanned granny on the first floor of my apartment building, half-crooning at me in her gutteral Fukushima dialect to make weather smalltalk. *Adzē nā?* Yes, ma'am, it *is* hot. Goddamn, is it hot.

I wanted to cry and found that I couldn't. If there is an appropriate soundtrack to this desperate, empty feeling, we have all heard it as Lavos spirals down to our eventual peril—"At the Bottom of Night." There not even sadness can survive. It is just a vast, starry emptiness.

•

2300 AD. The Day of Lavos has come and gone, and the instigator of this apocalypse has long departed. Back to space, perhaps, to inhabit another world elsewhere in the universe. Guru Belthasar's comments on the subject are ambiguous, and there is no sign of Lavos itself on the planet. Its spawn, however, remain on Death Peak where Lavos birthed them, destined to someday repeat the lifecycle of their progenitor. Mutants dominate broken urban landscapes. Robots patrol facilities long abandoned by mankind, programming and reprogramming themselves to KILL ALL HUMANS. These last human targets hole up in the temporarily safe but shattered dome cities. Lacking food, they hold onto life with the assistance of the Enertron, the rejuvenation device that does everything but sate the omnipresent gnawing hunger. The sweet water of prehistory has long dried up.

Crono, Lucca, and Marle arrive as three bright sprites in a world of dim earth-toned people. Trekking across a ruined laboratory, the party arrives at the Arris Dome. Doan, the community elder, is amazed at the gumption of these young strangers. As we later find out, he may well have just met his own distant grandparents.

Defeating a guardian robot in the corridors beneath the Dome, the party discovers a cache of spoiled food in a refrigeration unit long since failed. A corpse crumpled against the wall—the last person to attempt a trip below before our heroes arrive—is holding on to something small in his stiff hands—a single seed. In a nearby chest, a note—a clue!—probably written by this unlucky person, leads Crono and company to "the secret of this dome," an information center.

Computer-illiterate Marle fiddles with this complex technological wonder. Rather than accidentally summoning another guardian boss, Marle accesses a video recording of the Day of Lavos. Brief and occasionally staticky, the video feed shows an eruption of molten rock into the world of 1999 AD, shortly followed by Lavos itself. A plume of fiery quills shoots off from its body in all directions. Red destruction rains down from the sky. The video fizzles out. Lucca is nonplussed. Marle is stricken. Crono is characteristically silent.

"This…" Marle sputters, "…this can't be the way the world ends…"

•

This is the way the world ends
Not with a bang but a whimper.

The oft-quoted final lines of T.S. Eliot's "The Hollow Men" are echoed in Marle's outraged and desperate words. But Marle is both correct and incorrect.

If we fight Lavos and lose, we are "treated" to a special ending, and a horrific one at that. In that same information center in the Arris Dome in 1999 AD, three technical operators witness Lavos's ascension firsthand. All over the flattened world map red alerts flare. Then, a view of the earth—first a brilliant blue and green, then a foreboding, angry dark red. Then, gray. Superimposed over this holocaustic sight: "But… the future refused to change."

But this is not the way the world ends. Not exactly. Lavos's explosive rise has destroyed much of the world and seems to have decimated the population. (To be fair, the world of *Chrono Trigger* seems dangerously underpopulated in *every* era.) Humanity still survives, albeit in meager and threatening conditions. If these humans are doomed to die—and I think we can safely interpret Marle's idea of "the end of the world" to mean the extinction of mankind—then it will definitely occur with a whimper. The whimper of the last human to be exterminated by Mother Brain's robot hunters. The last woman to be left for dead by a marauding mutant. The last man to fall over dead from sickness and hopelessness.

But, does "the world" continue? Whether or not Crono is able to defeat Lavos, the players of *Chrono Trigger* have no assurance of what will happen in 2301 AD or beyond. But of course Crono can defeat Lavos. Because *we do*.

•

Returning safely from the enemy-infested tunnels beneath Arris Dome, Crono and party present the seeds—yes, they have apparently multiplied on the trip back to the surface—to Doan and his group. Although skeptical, Doan tells the party that his people will plant the seeds. They might just save their future.

Will these seeds thrive in the poisoned world of 2300 AD? Maybe not. But when Crono and his friends succeed in their mission to prevent the Day of Lavos, there will be no dark future for humanity at all. The game spares us the messy paradoxes that often accompany time travel and shows Doan surviving the timeline shift created by the removal of Lavos from the future. Summoned to the castle one last time, Crono is greeted by the united representatives of the Guardia family tree, from Ayla's husband Kino who planted that first seed, branching all the way forward to Doan, who—in whatever timeline's future he is from—has discovered the will to continue living.

•

A counterpoint to Eliot: *Even if I knew the world would end tomorrow, I would continue to plant my apple trees.*

The internet attributes this apocryphal quotation and several variants of it to both the sainted Protestant reformer Martin Luther and the celebrated civil rights leader named in his honor. The debate over whether or not this quote is "real," though, has no bearing on its message of determination, courage, and hope.

I was never much of a believer in *hope*. *Hope* is an all too convenient word. *Hope* gets peddled to desperate people as the slick fiction that somehow life will provide for them. It *has* to! Right?

But hope isn't blind. Hope is optimism—a *cautious* optimism. Hope is the strength to struggle for life, even from the pits of abject despair. Hop collective will of our heroes to face the fearsome unknown and the frightening *very* known. Without effort, hope is meaningless.

It is either the height of insult or the most empathetic of encouragements to tell the people of Fukushima to continue to plant their apple trees. Fears of radioactive produce have devastated the farms of this agricultural region. Apples, once a major celebrated produce of the Fukushima prefecture, no longer sell. But farmers must continue to plant their trees, because the only other choice is despair.

And there is actual hope. A few short years after the disaster, farms have begun to reclaim recently decontaminated land. The people and their government are not yet giving up, but progress will take hard work, many years, and a lot of seeds.

A seed is a future that might happen. No matter how carefully it may be tended and nurtured, it may never sprout. No matter how neglected or poorly sown, it may still take purchase and grow. The future in our world is not something we apprehend. We are forever glimpsing ahead to a moment that might never happen. We are the people of *Chrono Trigger*'s 2300 AD. All we can do is plant our seeds, work to nourish and encourage them, and hope they will someday grow into something beautiful, useful, alive.

NEUGA, ZIENA, ZIEBER, ZOM

North America does not experience the same continental catastrophology as the small island nation of Japan, completely contained in the Pacific Ocean's Ring of Fire. Indeed, natural disasters, which have been used as critical punctuation points in the run-on sentence of Japanese history, do not seem to preoccupy our transnational consciousness. In an instance of all-too-neat parallelism, the Tōhoku quake occurred on the eleventh day of March 2011. It wasn't long before media opportunists capitalized on the vocabulary of the September 11, 2001 attacks in the United States and dubbed the day "3/11," placing the tragedy on the same level as America's own go-to national crisis, 9/11. The succinct use of our own vocabulary conveys the import of the Great East Japan Earthquake far better than a lengthy explanation or even a "Simple English" Wikipedia page. By a simple substitution of terms, we can eliminate the *foreignness*, the *over-thereness*. We create an emotional response that makes sense to *us*, the locals.

•

The localizations of games produced in Japan have been a mixed bag. Misspellings and solecisms abound in early Nintendo games, like the *Ghosts 'n Goblins* farewell message "Congraturation this story is happy end," or *Pro Wrestling*'s "A winner is you!" A mixture of disdain and ironic appreciation often accompanies these sloppy translations. Others have become beloved exemplars of "Engrish." Meme historians among us will recall the viral line "All your base are belong to us," even if few of them played its source game, *Zero Wing*. Fans of the Squareverse, meanwhile, have a great affection for what is the most memorable insult of the first North American incarnation of *Final Fantasy IV*—"You spoony bard!"

All of these quirky translations have one thing in common—they were produced by Japanese speakers who knew English, but not quite well enough. Accurate, organic translations require native speakers of the target language to be present and engaged in the process. But sometimes translation alone doesn't suffice. Allusions to events, characters, imagery, and other artifacts specific to Japanese culture may not make sense across national borders, no matter how crisply they have been rendered into English.

If these borders are obstacles to clarity, then the process of localizing Japanese games—of masking "cultural odors" with Anglophone-friendly scents— takes place in what art historian and anthropologist Christopher Steiner deems a "border zone," a place in which "mediators wrestle with and negotiate the meaning and value that goods will assume when they 'land.'" *Chrono Trigger* has had the uncommon experience of being pushed through such border zones twice—first for its initial release onto the SNES, and a second time for its Nintendo DS port. And anyone who's entered (or re-entered) America's borders knows that crossing through customs can be a harrowing experience.

•

Scholar of Japanese literature Ted Woolsey had just completed his master's thesis on Japanese disasters in modern literature when he was hired to work for Square. Woolsey's first project was to work on the localization of what was to become *Final Fantasy Legend III*—the first Square title to feature an actual native English speaker at the helm of the translation—and his job was to make the English version as un-spoony as possible. Woolsey served as a translator for other seminal Square titles like *Secret of Mana*, *Final Fantasy III* (i.e. *FF6*), and of course, *Chrono Trigger*.

Woolsey's liberal use of familiar Western allusions at the expense of the Japanese source text has evoked both praise and derision from generations of Square fans. The term "Woolseyism" has even been coined, perhaps disparagingly, to describe translations that drastically divert from the Japanese original. Certainly the *Chrono Trigger* I played is keenly different from the one released in Japan.

Throughout their first decade and a half in North America, Nintendo was a fierce bowdlerizer of video games, both local and imported from Japan. References to "adult" themes in Japanese games—sex, nudity, violence, or alcohol—were expunged and often replaced with less objectionable material. So, no matter how fiercely devoted Square fans are to textual fidelity, Woolsey can surely be forgiven for keeping the Naga-ette Bromide ambiguously unsexual, or for turning a drinking contest into a soda-chugging game.

Beyond retooling scripts to fit Nintendo's standards, Woolsey added much of his own characteristic flair. For instance, he changed the names of Magus's three generals, Binegā, Soisō, and Mayonē to Ozzie, Slash, and Flea respectively. The astute reader might recognize those original names as Japanized versions of "vinegar," "soy sauce," and "mayonnaise," and indeed names as food puns are a staple of Akira Toriyama characters. In English, however, the Toriyama connection loses its impact, as does the phonetic resonance of having each of the names end in a long vowel. Similarly, it loses the pun of Flea/Mayonē ending his sentences with the compound particle *yonē*, which expresses both certainty and a desire to be validated—and an idiosyncrasy which makes Flea sound a bit "girlier." Woolsey replaced these linguistically nuanced condiments with references to rock musicians: vocalist Ozzy Osbourne, guitarist Slash of Guns N' Roses, and bassist Flea of Red Hot Chili Peppers. Elsewhere in the village of Dorino in 600 AD, Woolsey's joke gets a punch line when a villager calls Magus's generals "tone-deaf evil fiends." And, whether intentional or not, Ozzie's memorable exclamation "Ozzie's in a pickle!" plays on his Japanese name, while "Ozzie's in a jam!" deliciously puns on both.

Other Woolsey inventions are the frequent religious references. He renamed the lackluster *Majinki* ("Demon Machine") to the more familiar Mammon Machine, suggesting the biblical scale of the greed that drives Queen Zeal to madness. As for Queen Zeal's three cronies, the 1960s *Batman* henchmanesque names of Bosshu, Gasshu, and Hasshu were redubbed as Melchior, Gaspar, and Belthasar, the names traditionally given to the Christian Wise Men, or Magi, who visited the newly-born Jesus. Magi, of course, is a plural of "magus."

Some of Woolsey's translations seem purely fanciful. Magus's spell to summon Lavos was translated from the nonsensical "Da zuma rafua rō raira" to the equally gibberish "Neuga, zicna, zieber, zoм." But this too is purposeful, as it creates a rhyming couplet with the line, "Now the chosen time has come." Even this gobbledygook got localized to conform with English literatures's love for incantatory rhyme.

Perhaps Woolsey's biggest move was giving Frog the archaic knightspeak that defined his character for English audiences. In Japanese, Frog is actually the *least* proper of the party, ending his sentences with rough masculine particles like *ze* and *zo*, sounding more like a cartoonish thug than a medieval hero. Rendering this roughness into English might have necessitated the use of swear words, and you can guess how Nintendo of America would have felt about that.

Woolsey has been interviewed several times over the years on a broad range of topics, from his days at Square to his short run at video game company Big Rain, to his current work at Microsoft. I reached out to him with some questions of my own, and I was delighted to know that nearly two decades later Woolsey still remembers *Chrono Trigger* fondly.

•

Michael P. Williams: You've noted in several interviews the technical challenges, time limitations—you only had 30 days each to complete *Secret of Mana* and

Final Fantasy III—and censorship imposed on you in translating for North American Nintendo customers. What difficulties did localizing *Chrono Trigger* present?

Ted Woolsey: I was asked to do what I had to in order to improve the screen text after it had been given a rough translation by the staff. Essentially, I had to rewrite the game, and retranslate huge chunks. I spent several weeks in Tokyo, and later in Seattle, doing just that. It might have been that Square management at the time underestimated the complexity of translating *Chrono Trigger*, or games in general. They certainly fixed things in later years, hiring great, talented professionals to do the work and giving them some freedom and the right resources. But my work on *Chrono Trigger* was during the early days of SNES carts, and you had to hold so much of the story, voice, and tone in your head, imagining how characters would be interacting. It was hard trying to come up with resourceful solutions to some of the characters. I wish I had had more time to really think through some of my decisions. But in translating, sometimes you have to pick your North Star, and just run with it, especially when time is of the essence.

MPW: You added some flair to details, like Frog's Middle English grammar, and you injected some humor into the game, such as redubbing the Knights of Guardia the "Knights of the Square Table." Were there any instances where you resisted the urge to add more wordplay or humor?

TW: Looking back I probably could have pulled back on some of the language play. When I was doing that I sort of just channeled the original text, letting my brain play with the concepts—I can't say I was always happy with what came out in English, and certainly I pulled back a ton of shaping as the game cartridge didn't have the capacity for text overages. We had to cut to the bone.

With Frog, I just realized that while he had an interesting tone in Japanese, it seemed slightly too close to the other characters conversationally. I felt like he was a heroic type, and I tried to amp that up a bit.

MPW: What was your translation support team like?

TW: We had several people working on the memory map, and how to rework the ROM to accommodate English, and other languages like French and German. Other folks worked on graphics changes for localization. The folks who took a stab at translating *Chrono Trigger* were doing their first game—that can be tough, and I didn't mind jumping in to shape the final vision.

MPW: You've said that localizing names can be an exercise in re-exoticizing. Taking names like *Final Fantasy VI*'s "Tina" and making them more otherworldly, like "Terra."

TW: Yes, Square liked purely Western names because they would stand out in the text as exotic. I felt that using the same names in English, in some cases, lost the punch and exoticization of the original.

MPW: What level of communication did you have with Tom Slattery, who revised your translation for the DS? How do you feel about the game being given a revision of your own script, versus a retranslation of the original Japanese?

TW: None. I met Tom after the fact, and feel he did a great job as torchbearer! In some perverse way I'm glad the game includes pieces of my original work. I spent hundreds of hours working on it, and I loved chasing solutions to tough grammatical puzzles in the original text. That is the fun of translating—being resourceful, and doing your best to come up with concepts that help audiences pull as much out of the game as possible.

MPW: What were your working conditions like at Square? Were you integrated into the regular staff offices or were you treated like a guest or consultant?

TW: I was usually given an office space somewhere around where the "remake" staff was situated, so basically, just a cubicle like everyone else. For the most part, this was fine, though there were some occasions where I felt like I was sort of camping in a space where some folks didn't want me. I used standard issue computers with full access to required files via their file sharing system. I could come and go as I wished, but usually I was on a crazy deadline, so I was often working at the office ten hours or more a day.

MPW: Was *Chrono Trigger* an obvious choice for North American release, or did you lobby for this game?

TW: *Chrono Trigger* was a beautiful game, but certainly there were issues. The biggest one was the price of the ROM. *Chrono Trigger* would be the most expensive SNES game ever when it shipped, and I recall there being quite a bit of discussion around what that would do to sales. In the end, the company decided that the opportunity was sufficiently worthwhile, and proceeded with the game, but certainly business strategy played a large role in what games came to the US.

MPW: Were there games you vetoed for localization in favor of others, or games you backed but never made it to the States?

TW: I never really vetoed any of the Square-developed games, including *Front Mission*. Unfortunately, the business strategists felt that certain games would not be successful outside of Japan, or that they would be too costly to localize. I backed most of the products being produced in Japan, but ultimately Square management decided which titles they wanted to invest in localizing.

MPW: Did you have any influence on other games that were in development at Square while you were employed by them?

TW: I often saw games in early development, but I thought more about script design and story than other game elements. I often gave feedback when I was playing the Japanese version for things that would make the story more compelling or familiar. *Final Fantasy Mystic Quest* was ostensibly created just for non-Japanese audiences to train up more people on role-playing games—sort of an RPG on training wheels. That game needed tons of changes. Puzzles were too difficult, and the story was too awkward and too rooted in Japanese cultural themes. I spent quite a bit of time helping to shape that game. But even then I knew it was the wrong product to ship after *Final Fantasy II* (*FF4*) on the SNES. It just served as a letdown for customers who loved *Final Fantasy II*. I had translated around 75% of *Final Fantasy V* while *Mystic Quest* was in development, but I was told to shelve it until the market for RPGs was bigger. I really liked *FF5*, so that was super disappointing.

MPW: What influences did you draw upon in translating *Chrono Trigger*?

TW: I tried to draw on lots of styles of literature, comics and animated movies as the scenarios lent themselves to various treatments. There were some scatological or other humorous references in the Japanese version that I simply had to expunge or change. I think a lot of the translation was just following the original text and letting it flow through the filter, as it were. I had to radically cut down on the amount of text after the first couple of edits, so at some point, I just tossed the original aside and worked on shortening the version I had. Probably not the right thing to do, but at that point I was under the gun, and deleting extra words in a sentence actually mattered.

At some points I tried to inject some humor—in retrospect not universally appreciated!—when I felt the tale was dragging a bit. Also there were various writers for the Japanese version, each with a slightly different editorial voice, so I tried to play with some of that for ideas.

MPW: You used more than a few religious references absent in the original Japanese but very prominent in the North American translation. As a result, many players of the North American version have read more allegory into the game than the original story aimed for, but which are now permanent fixtures in the game's legacy here.

TW: Interesting that you point that out. I didn't really have the idea to turn the story into a biblically-laced horrorfest, but some of those terms and concepts contain charged, intense pearls of emotions that were helpful to amp up certain themes in the game. There certainly was an "end of days" component to the game's ending(s), and eons rather than centuries being considered in the game's timeline, so some of the imagery and concepts from Western religious traditions seemed to work. I wish it had been more purposeful, but again when you're channeling that much text, and characters are saying different things when they are selected for individual story arcs, a lot of what came out in the English was just what bubbled up almost unconsciously in my head while supporting and driving the story.

•

Woolsey's translation of *Chrono Trigger* remained intact when it was ported to the PlayStation in the *Final Fantasy Chronicles* collection, but just over thirteen years later, when it was chosen to be re-ported to the Nintendo DS, the translation was given a bit of an overhaul.

Tom Slattery's work for Square largely comprised new English translations of *Final Fantasy* games, including *FF6*—already translated once by Woolsey—and a 3D remake of *FF4*. Clearly aware of the fans' desire for something spoony in that game, Slattery retained that famous line, and even joked about it in his meta appearance in the in-game Developer's Office. Slattery's approach to retranslating games has been one filled with a desire to preserve the legacy established by previous editions, while eliminating unintentional mistakes and compensating for the technological problems posed by earlier versions. Woolsey, for example, was limited by character space, and thus names and items that would have fit comfortably in phonetically compact Japanese *katakana* needed truncation in English. This same limitation did not apply to Slattery, who was able to use lengthy terms like "Athenian water" over the shortened "revive." Slattery was also free of the draconian censorship under which the first North American release of *Chrono Trigger* chafed.

Slattery graciously answered some questions I had about his work on *Chrono Trigger*, shining some light on how Square and its localizations have changed since the SNES days.

•

Michael P. Williams: What was it like to retranslate games you grew up with, specifically Woolsey-translated games?

Tom Slattery: On the one hand, having the opportunity to update so many of these games that defined my childhood for a new generation was a dream come true. On the other hand, knowing that fans would compare each and every word to the original—that there would be some people upset by any line that changed, and others upset by any that didn't—made it quite a daunting task. I did my best to strike a balance between preserving nostalgia and providing the best experience possible for new players, but there are of course people who felt the retranslations went too far in one direction or the other.

It was definitely interesting reading and working in the same files Woolsey had translated years before, though. Seeing what he had to deal with—and without the benefit of Google, Wikipedia, and dedicated fan sites that analyze every minute detail of the games like I had—certainly gives you a renewed appreciation for what he was able to accomplish in such a short time. There are conversations that are completely scrambled in the files, messages that get reused without warning, messages that don't show up at all, and of course no comments whatsoever to provide a translator with clues to any of those things.

MPW: Woolsey has been criticized for his translation decisions, but ultimately these translations became the standard text of the games in North America, and deviations from them might ruin the nostalgia factor. Which "Woolseyisms" did you want to retain for *Chrono Trigger*, and what elements did you want to bring closer to the Japanese original?

TS: Many of the other ports and remakes I worked on received fully new translations, but with *Chrono Trigger* it was more along the lines of an update and polishing pass. It's probably easier to talk about the things I wanted to change than the ones I wanted to preserve.

My main goals were to undo the damage done by the character limits of the original version and to eliminate the inconsistencies that weakened the game's settings and characterizations. I expanded the enemy, item, and ability names that had clearly been compressed or altered to fit within the artificial length restrictions of the SNES release, but I retained virtually all of the character names. With dialogue, I worked from the existing text and mostly tried to tighten up what Ted had done. I loved the caveman speak of Ayla and friends, for example, but it drifted around quite a bit. Sometimes they used articles and plurals, and sometimes they didn't. Sometimes their subjects and verbs agreed, and other times they didn't. I loved that Frog didn't sound like the characters from present day, but it made no sense that he was the only character in his time period with an anachronistic style of speech, and the grammar wasn't consistent or even always used correctly.

As with *Final Fantasy VI*, I tried to preserve the most nostalgic lines—except where they did things inappropriate to the setting, like referencing U.S. currency—and inject new humor where I could. At least from my perspective, though, *Chrono Trigger* didn't really have as many memorable one-liners as *Final Fantasy VI*. Even being a fan of both games, I did a lot of digging when working on them to see which aspects of the localization other players were attached to, and while *Final Fantasy VI* was a very quotable game, it seemed that for most people *Chrono Trigger*'s charm came more from the overall story and character interactions than from individual lines. Because of that, I was fairly liberal with changes to dialogue. If I thought something was an improvement, I generally went with it.

MPW: Did you add any "Slatteryisms" to the game?

TS: Here and there, for sure. I turned the "soup" in prehistory into "skull-smash" (because "next day, skull feel like smash!"), for example, and turned a line where a child doesn't understand a Japanese phrase meaning "generous" or "charitable" into one where she misunderstands the word "magnanimous," thinking that people are calling her father chubby.[11]

Of course, I introduced a couple of unintentional Slatteryisms as well.

Firstly, as many have noticed, I made Azala female with a single instance of a feminine pronoun. Azala

---

11   Slattery's joke reads: "Everybody says Daddy's magnanimous, but he says he's just big-boned."

was Ayla's nemesis, the name sounded completely feminine, and the sprite looked like it was wearing a flowing pink robe. My brain had so unquestioningly taken the character to be the reptite queen from the start that it had never even occurred to me she—I mean, it—might not be female. No one called out my assumption, and it wasn't until after the game had mastered up that I noticed there was no direct reference to the gender of any reptite in the game. They may have been intended to be genderless, or gender may simply not have been seen as an important detail considering they're not human, but the Japanese version always avoids specifying. I actually just did a bit of searching to see whether Japanese players had interpreted the character as male or female, and saw that the Japanese Wikipedia article currently states the character is "believed to be female because the English DS version refers to Azala as 'she.'" So I guess I've successfully confused Japan too.

Secondly, I translated the area that should have been the Darkness Beyond Time as "Time's Eclipse" in the new ending. No one had mentioned that the term was a *Chrono Cross* reference, so without a *Chrono Cross* glossary for reference and being unfamiliar with the Japanese version of the name—I'd played *Chrono Cross* in English—I had no reason to guess it wasn't a newly coined location name like all the others. Kind of a bummer that the reference was lost, though, since that sequence was meant to tie the two games together.

MPW: How did you approach translating new dialogue that was not in the original, like the new ending and the new sidequests?

TS: Translating the new text was honestly the easiest part of the project. It was the only place where I didn't have legacy to contend with; it was just a matter of matching the style and characterizations from the rest of the game. Of course, the added portions were also the last things to make it into the game, and content was changing up until the final day of quality assurance, so there were certainly translation challenges in that regard.

MPW: Did you face other technical challenges, time limitations, or censorship issues in retranslating for North American Nintendo customers?

TS: Only a couple of technical challenges come to mind. One was that the recycled anime cutscenes from the PlayStation version contained baked-in text overlays that couldn't be altered, meaning that any of the lines or terms they referenced—like the name of the sword Masamune—couldn't be changed in the DS release. Another was that recycled messages and substitution variables thwarted my attempt at making Robo sound more robotic. His characterization comes across less distinct in English than it does in Japanese, and I had explored using ALL CAPS as a way to bring it a little closer to the original, which uses *katakana* script on the verb endings to make it clear he sounds like a robot when he talks. That proved impossible, though, both because he shared some common lines with other characters and because there was no way to force capitalization on the variable strings that were inserted into dialogue, such as the names of party members. That was probably for the best, though. I IMAGINE IT WOULD HAVE BEEN A BIT OVER THE TOP AND I WOULD HAVE ABANDONED THE IDEA ANYWAY.

Time was definitely the biggest limiting factor. *Chrono Trigger DS* had the tightest schedule of any game I worked on at Square Enix. On a normal project, I'd be expected to translate somewhere around 2000 to 2500 Japanese characters per day; for *Chrono Trigger*, I needed to get through more like 5000 to 6000. That meant I had to focus on the areas I felt would benefit the most from the attention, and let some other things go. There was no time for researching creative historical speech patterns or iterating on dialogue; I had to work with the tools already in my toolbox.

Censorship wasn't an issue at all. I was never asked to change any aspect of the translation for ratings or any other reason. I used some common sense as a translator—softening some of the more overtly suggestive lines and outright references to alcohol in a way that would hopefully go over the heads of children—but that was more of a culturalization issue than one of censorship. Japanese and American cultural views on what is appropriate and inappropriate for children vary fairly drastically.

MPW: What was your translation/editorial support team like?

TS: It was basically a one-man operation for English. I had an editor, but really only serving in a copyediting capacity on this project—catching typos and whatnot. There were, however, some fantastic localization coordinators working behind the scenes to help. They played through virtually every sequence of the game with different party combinations and recorded them so I'd be able to check context and make sure the lines flowed correctly as translated. Given the tight schedule, I would have been flying blind without that. The nonlinear nature of the game, combined with free party formation and sequences that only occur when certain characters are present, would have made it impossible to check everything.

MPW: Do you think the target audience of the original SNES release differed from that of the DS version?

TS: Absolutely. But fans of the original version—much older by that time—were a major segment of the target audience for the DS version, as evidenced by the nostalgic "Good morning, Crono!" marketing campaign. Speaking of which, I wish someone had told me that campaign was going to happen. I wouldn't have changed the line in question if I'd known the game's website was going to be goodmorningcrono.com!

MPW: Were there any details from the original translation that felt out of date?

TS: The character limits were far and away the most outdated aspect of the localization. The overt censorship in things like "soup" and the "soda-guzzling contest" was another. Otherwise, the main thing that felt dated to me was the general lack of consistency in speech patterns and characterizations. It was miles beyond most other SNES games, and impressive given the time constraints of the original localization, but the bar has been raised since then.

MPW: If you had been the first translator of *Chrono Trigger* instead of Woolsey, what would you have done differently?

TS: The biggest thing I would have done differently would have been coining original names where the Japanese ones didn't work rather than introducing real-world references to pop culture, history, and Christian myth. I probably would have kept the sword Masamune named Grandleon as it was in the original Japanese. I might have tried to find a distinctive style of speech to distinguish 12,000 BC from 600 AD as well, time permitting. All in all, though, there isn't that much I would have done differently.

•

No matter what choices either Woolsey or Slattery made, however, there are fans who disagree with those choices. The fansite Chrono Compendium hosts the Chrono Trigger Retranslation Project, completed in March 2007 by user KWhazit. This new translation, staunchly faithful to the original Japanese, predates the release of Slattery's translation by more than a year and a half, and consequently does not include the new dialogue issued with the DS version.

The effort expended here is phenomenal, and its results are fascinating. Browsing the comparative lines of Woolsey, the original Japanese, and the new direct translation shows how much of the original had to be trimmed for space, and how much Woolsey reshaped the text. But there are also instances of text that sound like Engrish, no matter how faithful they are to the Japanese. "Shall I lecture about the damage you take during combat?" asks a helpful woman in the Mayor's house in Truce, according to KWhazit. Woolsey simply has her ask, "Want to learn about damage in battle?"[12]

As of 2011, players can experience *Chrono Trigger* on Apple's iOS and Android systems, in Japanese, English,[13] French, Italian, German, Spanish, Chinese, or Korean. With this multiplicity of "official" translations, we are given even more of a multicanonical perspective on *Chrono Trigger* where several things can be true at the same time, depending on which version of the game we've played. Add in the expanded storylines of semisequel *Radical Dreamers* and official mass-market sequel *Chrono Cross*, and there are more threads to tie together than any one player can handle alone.

Luckily, the success of *Chrono Trigger* has spawned multiple generations of fans who have endeavored to explore and to re-explore the games and discuss their theories with passion. But more practically, many of these Chrono experts provide help with a core element of *Chrono Trigger*—mastering the gameplay.

Replaying *Chrono Trigger* in 2013 was easy for me. Numerous text FAQs and YouTube playthroughs of the game exist, so I wasn't long without help when I

---

12 "戦闘中に受けるダメージについてレクチャーしましょうか?"

13 The Slattery translation, with slightly modified instructional dialogue to account for a touchscreen, rather than a controller.

had forgotten how to defeat a golem or where to find the Black Rock. But back in 1995, before I had reliable internet access and before the age of Google, there were precious few resources when I was stuck at an impasse. Often my only advisors were the teasingly small and occasionally inaccurate instruction manuals packaged with games. But for *Chrono Trigger* and a select few other titles, I had a secret weapon—a library of strategy guides.

LIFE BY THE BOOK

I ADORE BOOKS.

I love the tactile thrill of pages thrumming my thumb as I flip through a slick paperback, the textured tickle of an unjacketed clothbound hardcover. Even that *smell* of old library books, the acidified paper and mouldering paste intermingling into a bouquet of pungent wisdom. From my early days hunting through the mildewy basement of my great-grandfather's old print shop for loose ornithology plates, to present-day rummages through disorganized thrift store shelves, I have spent a lot of time looking for books. Collecting volumes of a series, placing them side by side, seeing a body of knowledge *grow*—a book-lover can easily become obsessed.

Of the many series of books I've collected and organized over my literate years, some of the most impactful and fascinating have been the *Nintendo Player's Guide* series. I read walkthroughs like they were novellas and I became an expert on games I'd never even play. Digests like the

NES Game Atlas begat omnibuses like *Mario Mania*, paving the way to expansive one-shot strategy guides for individual games. *Chrono Trigger Player's Guide* entranced me with the official manga artwork of Akira Toriyama and the quaint 3D maps of Gentarō Araki. Along with the official in-box manuals, these player's guides became not only companions to my gameplay, but also fuel for my imagination. Somewhere in my archive of collected drawings and writings dating back to my kindergarten days is a hand-drawn picture of *Chrono Trigger*'s Janus, dated 1998. Years after finishing games, I would keep coming back to their guides for more. These books were scriptures. And like any serious acolyte, I had trouble ignoring the insistent dicta of strategy guides.

•

The term "strategy guide" is a convenient misnomer, especially in the case of role-playing games. RPG strategy guides usually contain a mix of character dossiers, walkthroughs, cartographies, spellbooks, item manifests, and—my favorite!—bestiaries. Poor placement of these elements can easily turn a companion volume into a book of spoilers. Of course, overeager readers can spoil their own experience by peeking too far ahead.

Me, I was a boy scout gamer. I was always prepared for the challenges ahead. I kept an open guide handy when I needed directions in an expansive dungeon crawl. I didn't want to miss anything. I wanted to collect every single item, whether unique relic or mundane tonic. I just couldn't abide the idea of flying blind. Of an incomplete performance.

My game scout sash had a special merit badge for rampant cheating. Although I was a straight-A student who never cheated in school, I felt no compunction about using cheat cartridges like the Game Genie. I rarely called upon this powerful djinn until after I had completed the game "fairly," or had failed miserably to do so. Just like in school, I wanted the sense of completion that came from hard work, even if it meant hours of homework—grinding for hours for level-ups and gold. With some irony, I regret not having devoted the same level of effort to improving my own physical fitness and economic situation in real life.

Most of the Game Genie codes readily available for players of *Chrono Trigger* were less visual novelties than they were in-game steroids. So, rather than hacking the game to replace Gato's sprite with racebot Johnny's, or to open up unused maps for exploration, you could begin the game with maximum stats and all techs learned, obviating the need for grinding. Or, you could activate the "one-hit kill" code, and win every battle instantly no matter who strikes first. Apply the "walk through walls" code, and now you are an invincible demigod unfettered by the limits of space. This last code is a great way to break the game—take a transoceanic stroll and enter an area earmarked for much later in the game, and you find yourself hurtled forward in the game's progress, unable to complete objectives now required for further adventuring. Congratulations, cheater. You fucked up.

I learned these lessons the hard way in my most recent playthroughs of *Chrono Trigger*. The second time I ventured through the game as an adult, I had specific objectives in mind. One of the most arduous goals I had set for myself was the tedious, maddening, and ultimately imperfect quest to count every single human character in the game. I needed shortcuts, and I had the means to take them.

We humans often operate as if we're on a level playing field where everyone has the same opportunities for professional, romantic, economic, and physical success—an assumption that's as comforting as it is false. No matter what weapons Marle holds or how high she levels up, she will never be as physically strong as Crono. And no matter how hard he trains or begs magic master Spekkio, Crono can never learn the healing spells that are Marle's natural talents. So why not give our characters the best we can, and max up their levels and stats so high that the game displays them as "★★"? Is it unethical to speed up the game to make our level 1 nobodies into star-studded superheroes?

Just to complicate things, I suggest that the very premise of *Chrono Trigger*—hacking the timestream to achieve our desires—is cheating.

•

No matter what altruism supports our monkeying with history, we arrogantly assume the duties and privileges of a chronarchy, deriving our authority from the blessings of three doddering gurus who have lost touch with everyday NPCs. Granted, many of our objectives are arguably for the greater good, even if they cause collateral damage. Our goal to defeat Lavos saves humankind and much of organic life, though it is at the expense of Lavos's children and perhaps much of the potential inorganic—that is, robotic—life in 2300 AD. Our quest to achieve Fiona's green dream of a forested south continent ignores the delicate ecosystem of the desert that supports the sandmermannish "mohavors" and crustaceanlike "hexapods." Sure, these things are living creatures, but they're also *monsters*. So we judge our activities to be good—as corrections to history for the sake of humankind.

Other alterations to the timeline are even more self-interested. We willfully alter history to change the personality of the acquisitive 1000 AD mayor of Porre, so that we can take the Sun Stone from a more generous version of him. Just like the original mayor, we only want the Sun Stone for our own material benefit. Or is it because of the off chance that those materials we fashion from the Sun Stone will give us an extra edge against Lavos? Greater good, fine. We also have a unique chance to save Lucca's mom from paralysis, a mulligan that no one else on the globe gets. Is the act of de-disabling Lara part of this nebulous greater good, or is it a selfish life hack?

Regardless of what our actions in the timestream are, not only do we willfully violate every single directive of time travel that sci-fi history has urged us to respect, but we do it with the justification that *we are heroes*. We have appointed ourselves masters of time, and wielding our Gate Key like a five-pointed scepter, we decree who gets saved and who doesn't.

Of course, if we believe, as the game suggests, that some greater *Entity*—the spirit of the world itself?— created the disruptions in time so that someone would take advantage of them, then why shouldn't it be Crono and company who seize the opportunity? Why shouldn't Lucca travel through that mysterious red gate and save her mother from harm? It could easily have been a party of treasure hunter Toma, Elaine the merchant's daughter, Tata the wannabe knight, and mystic prodigy Schala who were brought together by circumstances beyond their control to serve the Entity's purposes. Were these other worthies cheated by the Entity, then, by not receiving the chance to be heroes? Or is it pure dumb luck that Crono and company end up saving the world?

•

The manual packaged along with *Chrono Trigger* takes us only so far, leaving us right in the aftermath of having defeating Yakra, the game's first true boss. The guide ends with an advertisement for *Chrono Trigger Player's Guide* at a reasonable retail price of $14.95. Just call 1-800-255-3700 to pre-order! Today, that 800 number still leads to Nintendo, though I'm certain the *Chrono Trigger Player's Guide* went out of print years ago.

This *Player's Guide* was released by Nintendo in October 1995, a few months after the game's North American debut. Billed on the cover as "the complete guide to the past, present and future—straight from the pros at Nintendo," the large-format guide in fact leaves much unsaid. Unlike the colorful early strategy guides from Japan, *Chrono Trigger Player's Guide* is a mostly no-nonsense document. There are no illustrated bestiaries, no bonus comics, no interviews, and no mail-in prize giveaways. And a later unofficial guide from BradyGames published to coincide with the PlayStation port feels more like a technical report than a companion for playtime.

The release of the DS version in North America, even with its fresh translation and new features, did not seem to necessitate a new guide. Was this one sign of the growing irrelevance of the print strategy guide in an ever-growing digital world of capable walkthroughs, FAQs, and YouTube speedruns? While BradyGames and competitor Prima Games are still printing titles, these books look increasingly more "deluxe"—manufactured collector's items that are closer to souvenirs than actual gameplay aids. Perhaps this is the way of bookkind in general. No longer the primary means of the storage and transmission of culture, books may become *objets d'art*, physical novelties prized more as museum pieces than as carriers of information. I myself have resorted to using digital substitutes for some of the titles explored in this chapter.

Yes, I can only scroll through the scanned pages of my first direct bibliographic link to *Chrono Trigger* to reacquaint myself with the kind of in-depth light reading my 1990s self found so fascinating. I notice something on the back cover of that manual—well, the last page of the PDF scan. "Square Soft Customer Service/Game Counseling." Automated service 24 hours a day, and live operators available Monday through Friday, 9 to 5.

I never once dialed 206-861-0303. Here in the 215 area code way on the other coast, that was a long-distance call, one I couldn't hide on the family's itemized phone bill. Today, I brave the chance that this number will lead me to an angry resident, sick of getting pranked by nostalgic Squareheads. The phone rings.

Boo ba beep!

This number—much like the Game Counseling Department, I imagine—is no longer in service.

•

Long before I was pencilling off-model manga characters from *Chrono Trigger*, I was still drawing video game stuff. My *Gray's Anatomy* was a collection of Nintendo game manuals—*Mega Man*, *The Legend of Zelda*, *Super Mario Bros. 2*. These booklets were an endless source of inspiration and reference for my doodling, and for my obsessive-compulsive desire to list, to categorize, and to catalog. No wonder I ended up working in a library.

The most fascinating and numerous of the inhabitants of these slim booklets were the monsters and the villains. Over the years I've collected bestiaries of all types—humorous and rhyming abecedarians by new cryptozoologists like Edward Lear and Dr. Seuss, and monstrous compendia straight from the Wizards of the Coast, those littoral literati responsible for keeping dungeons full of dragons since 1997. All of these sources say the same thing—*Monsters are all around you, so here is what you need to know.*

Chrono Trigger's monsters often skew on the side of cutesy. Many of them would look just fine palling around with any of the totally-not-Pokémon alternate-Toriyamaverse *Dragon Quest Monsters*. Unlike the lovable baddies of the Dragon Quest series or the high-fantasy foes of the Final Fantasy games, *Chrono Trigger*'s monsters don't spontaneously manifest from the ether for a random encounter. We can often see them ahead, assuming we look closely enough. Sometimes they get the drop on us, having waited in ambush. Or they may amble around aimlessly until we pass into their field of vision. Some monsters make an almost choreographed entrance to the fight, twirling in and issuing battle cries. The integrated map and battle screen interface of *Chrono Trigger* emphasizes a chilling truth of life—*Danger is right in front of you, and sometimes you can't avoid it.*

When we fight, though, we are paralyzed. While our enemies mill about the battle screen, we are stuck in place. Unlike spiritual predecessor *Secret of Mana*, *Chrono Trigger* does not let us move around the battlefield. We can only stand and fight, or run away in fear.

So we grind. Because if we skip too many fights, sooner or later we're going to get caught off guard and killed. We learn new techs and magic, discovering latent talents every couple of levels. But this one-sided approach ignores the practical advice of that patron of military strategists, Sun Tzu: *Know thy enemy.* We have neither a quick-reference Pokédex nor the convenient Peep or Libra spells of the *Final Fantasy* universes to give us on-demand stats and weaknesses for our foes.

If we don't have a strategy guide, the best we've got is the in-game Sight Scope, which lets us view non-boss enemy hit points. But this item is only equippable at the expense of another stat-boosting or resistance-granting accessory. Because it's impossible to wear a ring, a bracelet, an amulet, and a pair of sunglasses at the same time.

Chrono Trigger mostly forces us to go into battle as a team. Since we fight side by side, the best options usually involve working together. Double and triple techs are often more efficient solutions than making our party whale on enemies with individual attacks. And cooperate we should, because our enemies are doing the same! The winged "cave apes" of 65,000,000 BC pick up the mushroom-like "shists" and hurl them at the party. Deep in the Ocean Palace in 12,000 BC, cyclopean "scouts" and their blue and red cousins will team up to deliver a powerful shadow magic attack. Since enemies also use rudimentary double and triple techs against the party, we've got to fight fire with fire. Well, probably water.

No matter how prepared we are, no matter how beefed up our party is, we can still have our heads handed to us. Some enemies have attacks that are debilitating at any level. The Iron Orb attack favored by Zealish pretender Dalton and his golem cronies will halve a party member's hit points in one shot. And when encountering "nu" in the wild, we have to watch out for a headbutt that reduces a character's HP to 1. Even if we are able to defeat our opponents, they may have a final counterattack waiting to twist our potentially Pyrrhic victory into a bitter loss. The fact that enemies have attacks altogether indifferent to our hard-earned experience reveals a hard lesson—*No matter how high your station in life, you can always be brought low.*

•

To thirteen-year-old me, playing *Chrono Trigger* without a strategy guide would have been equal parts thrilling and terrifying. But I made my first adult replay of the game a closed book affair. Mainly because I don't have a copy of *Chrono Trigger Player's Guide* anymore, except as a PDF. So what if I didn't find that Magic Tab on Mt. Woe? So what if I forgot to literally charm the pants off Ozzie and obtain his rare slacks? Learning to let go of perfection, to embrace uncertainty and spontaneity, has been a difficult point of personal growth for me. My transformation from a boy who plays by the book to a man who makes his own rules is far from complete.

Many of our contemporaries crave strategy guides for their lives. I see commuters on the subway reading well-highlighted Christian devotionals. And when their pages are completely soaked through with yellow, new books will replace them. On the secular side, *The Seven*

Habits of Highly Effective People has been superseded by *The 8th Habit: From Effectiveness to Greatness*. And souls of every race, creed, color, occupation, and age group can rest assured that if they don't have the book version of a bowl of chicken soup, one will be out of the kitchen soon enough to soothe them.

We can find help for our problems in books, but we cannot become slaves to their words. We need to live our lives, not imagine how they could be if only we had the *The Power of Positive Thinking*, or some hidden ancient *Secret* to making our dreams come true. We need to *do something*.

We only have so many years to live, and there just isn't enough time.

THE END OF TIME

Even though I've been writing about a game whose *raison d'être* is time travel, it's taken me a long time to get around to discussing it.

Chrono Trigger was certainly not the first video game to employ time travel. It wasn't even the first Square RPG to do so by far. The first *Final Fantasy* features a red-haired fighter and friends eventually unsealing a magical "time gate" to defeat a nefarious villain lurking in the past, and *Final Fantasy Legend III* explores the power of time-machine-powered travel to prevent disaster in past, present, and future eras. *Chrono Trigger* ups the ante by using time travel to flirt with genres as disparate as prehistoric fiction, medieval fantasy, and post-apocalyptic sci-fi. *Chrono Trigger*'s immediate Square predecessor, *Live A Live*, presages such genre-bending by featuring not only a caveman hero and a futuristic robot, but also other representatives of genre fiction: a knight, a ninja, and a cowboy. The game even has a villain called Maō, which some of you might recognize as the Japanese name for Magus.

Chrono Trigger combines the successes of both *Final Fantasy Legend III* and *Live A Live*, making time travel both integral to the story and historically comprehensive. Time travel seems so deeply enmeshed in the plot that it's difficult to imagine the game without it. Blasphemous as it may sound, however, I believe that *Chrono Trigger* doesn't actually need time travel to be a successful game.

•

Hey.

I'm glad you picked this book back up after hurtling it across the room. Or maybe you just restarted your tablet after an indignant shutdown. What the fuck is this guy saying, that *Chrono Trigger* doesn't need time travel? *The word "chrono" is in the title!* Bear with me as I rephrase just slightly the plot summary I provided many chapters ago.

Crono, a teenage boy from a small town, his techno-savvy gal pal Lucca, and princess-in-disguise Marle end up opening a hole in the universe—a gate. *Discovering the link between their own world and others, the trio travels through different worlds assembling a party of allies: the knight-errant-turned-frog, Frog; stalwart robot Robo; rough-and-tumble cavewoman Ayla; and finally Magus, a dark sorcerer with mysterious allegiances. Learning that their worlds—that all life itself!—will be destroyed by Lavos, a sinister force from beyond, the septet travel onward, gathering clues and materials, meeting supporters, and battling foes to prepare themselves for that final, decisive battle for the future.*

There's no need for time travel to make this story happen. But, what about the disappearance of Queen Leene erasing Marle out of existence, for instance? Surely that plot point couldn't work here! I think it could. Let's imagine a multiverse a little like that of *The Legend of Zelda: A Link to the Past*. In this Zelda title—and many of its successors—two parallel worlds coexist. The Light World and the Dark World bear many similarities to each other in structure, and many locations have corresponding alternate versions in each universe. As Link, we warp between the worlds, solving puzzles that exploit the dichotomous nature of reality. Would it be preposterous to suggest that characters across universes could be affected by events in a world parallel—or even quasi-perpendicular—to their own? Of course that game just wouldn't be *Chrono Trigger*.

•

Time travel in *Chrono Trigger* is a messy affair. Lucca introduces us to its mechanics in 600 AD, shortly after Marle winks out of existence to "somewhere cold, dark… and lonely."

Delighted with her unintentional impersonation of Queen Leene, Marle gladly enjoys the comforts of a royal lifestyle where she is no longer treated as a ward of the king, but a queen in her own right. Let's ignore the creepy realization that at some point King Guardia XXI might try to have sex with his teenaged distant descendant. Meanwhile, the search for the real Leene is called off, since Marle is a dead ringer for her. Leene—along with the 600 AD Chancellor—never gets rescued, and is killed by Yakra and his minions. Maybe they ritually sacrifice her to the idol of Magus deep within the cathedral. Maybe they do much worse to her. She's a lot prettier than a naga-ette, after all. But to save Marle from this variation of the Grandfather Paradox, we must preserve Leene's place in the timestream. Sounds easy, right?

Not really.

If we do not rescue Leene, then Marle ceases to exist. If Marle had never been born, Crono would not have met her at the Millennial Fair, and Lucca's teleporter wouldn't have malfunctioned and created a time gate. But perhaps in this alternate timeline, there is no Guardia anymore. In 600 AD, the Mystics led by general Ozzie take advantage of the confusion following Leene's death, and push through the lines of defense at Zenan Bridge.

Without Crono and company to battle them, Ozzie's undead minions easily conquer the Knight Captain and his unmagical troops. The monster army storms Guardia. Banta and his young wife are slain—there will be no Taban, and thus no Lucca. There will be no Millennial Fair to celebrate a thousand unbroken years of monarchy, and no teleporter sideshow. No Crono to travel back in time. And of course, no Marle to have given him reason to in the first place.

But, wait.

Leene only dies because Marle's appearance causes the palace to call off the search. So in order for Leene to die, Marle must exist. But when Leene dies, her descendant Marle can't exist. If you'll allow the admixture, we're trapped in a sort of Schrödinger's catch-22 here, where both Marle and Leene must be both alive and dead to make this scenario work.

The events of this first exposition of time rules reveal another curious fact. Namely, Marle vanishes from the timeline *before Leene is even killed*. We have to save the living Queen Leene to recall the sort of dead Marle from the darkness beyond time. We do not recover a dead Leene and revive her, which, by the way, is a technology humans have always had. At 200G a pop, resurrection sells for fairly cheap. Since the royal family could easily spare this pittance, we must assume the morbid premise that Leene's body will never be found if she is killed.

The introduction to *Secret of Mana* tells us that "time flows like a river." Damming a river downstream won't cause water upstream to vanish. The current will weaken, the water will ebb, and the river will dry up. So, does time struggle upstream to keep up with changes closer to its source? This temporal quirk *sounds* like it might help explain the apparent subparadox of having Leene alive while Marle has vanished, but in fact it proves the opposite. If Marle had continued to play queen in 600 AD, Leene would have been killed, her remains left in an unmarked grave. Marle would have acted the part of Leene for a while longer, as time caught up with itself before finally disintegrating Marle from the timeline.

Remember that this Marle/Leene episode is our first taste of how time should operate in *Chrono Trigger*, and it's already a bit of a trainwreck. So it actually works in our favor that the rest of the game is not slavish to the infernal, niggling logic of causality.

For starters, ignoring paradoxes allows us to make changes to the timeline in the first place, raising the stakes for adventure without bogging *Chrono Trigger* down with complexities. It also sets up interesting puzzles, some of which flagrantly defy the Grandfather Paradox. Like those sealed chests in the Middle Ages and in the present. We shouldn't open those boxes in 600 AD, because we'll forfeit the chance in 1000 AD to get powered-up versions of the items they contain.

But if we unlock those same chests in the present, we can travel back to 600 AD, snag the contents, and effectively get two for the price of one. The universe does not implode if we grab both the Nova Armor in the Northern Ruins in 600 AD and its powered-up version, the Moon Armor, in 1000 AD. We can cheat the system a bit without any temporal repercussions.

Analyzing the ins and outs—more often than not, the *highs and lows*—of the time travel utilized in *Chrono Trigger*, is an exercise riddled with frustration, headaches, and overexplanations. In short, it is the height of nerdish joy.

The easiest answer to these logical inconsistencies is a simple one—*Chrono Trigger* is a game designed by committee. While the lead producers shared mutual enthusiasm, they also contributed their own individual inputs that did not necessarily match up to their colleagues'. Their staff, however, was forced to make everything work, even if it wasn't compatible with other content. Game supervisor Yūji Horii, for example, sketched out a basic plot in which "a character would travel to the past, make some actions, and that would change the current or future situation of the character." Meanwhile producer Hironobu Sakaguchi designed monsters and characters like Gato struggling for inclusion. Even Akira Toriyama's concept art needed to be worked into the game. That iconic Toriyama image of Crono battling in the snow with Frog and Marle at his side, for example, wasn't even implemented until late in *Chrono Trigger*'s production, when programmers found a place in the story for Death Peak.[14] Worse, this image is simply *wrong*. Marle uses water magic, not fire. And this image was the box art—the very first thing players saw! Toriyama admitted that he was supposed to have drawn an ice sword, but it was too difficult for him so he substituted flame instead. Story planner Masato Katō, who wrote the entire Kingdom of Zeal scenario, recalled later that developing *Chrono Trigger* "wasn't exactly 'smooth sailing,' and a lot of the parts ended up being changed in the end."[15] Despite all of Katō's additions and editing, he was not included as an honorary Dream Teamer.

For those looking for in-game solutions to time travel problems, the folks at Chrono Compendium have compiled many excellent theories on the whys and why-nots of time mechanics in *Chrono Trigger*, and even introduced some of their expanded mechanics in their unofficial interquel to *Chrono Trigger* and *Chrono Cross*,

---

14 Death Peak—and probably the Crono Clone sidequest— had not yet been created at the time of the "Perfect Interview," later included in *Kurono Torigā Kōryaku Daitokushū*.
15 "トリガーも難航してね、終盤トップがすげかえられちゃったんだよね。"

a fangame called *Crimson Echoes*. One such intriguing theory is something they call Time Traveler's Immunity.

•

While we can conveniently ignore time travel paradoxes, we can't ignore how our actions in time seem to affect others without affecting us. Well, except for that whole Marle thing. Anyway, *except for that whole Marle thing which is supposed to explain how time travel in* Chrono Trigger *works*, time travel in *Chrono Trigger* might actually work by bestowing immunity to the effects of time travel upon those who travel through time. Except for Marle that one time.

The most heartbreaking example involving immunity is Lucca's chance to prevent Lara from injury in 590 AD. Assuming Lucca does rescue her mother, Lara will have lived her life perfectly ambulatory, probably forgetting how close to paralysis she had come. But Lucca will always remember that she had changed her past so profoundly. Does Lucca then have the unique experience of having been raised by both disabled and *en*abled versions of Lara? Or does she only remember the paraplegic mother who sat alone by the window upstairs? Either way, this is a difficult position for Lucca. If she remembers both childhoods at once, she may experience trauma or even madness from her conflicting but equally real memories. On the other hand, if she doesn't acquire memories of Lara as an able-bodied mother, then not only is she cheated out of the very childhood she thought she was saving, but her memories are now incompatible with those of her loved ones. The only authentic memories she can share with Lara and Taban are those events that occurred before Lara's potential accident. Our PCs—and by extension, anyone else who has time-traveled—are not just skipping around on the greater timeline, but now also following their own personal timelines.

As our party travels backward and forward through time, their bodies do not simply stop aging. Traveling back in time does not obliterate them into their formative molecules, and traveling to the future does not turn them into the dust they'll one day become. Our party actively ages as they complete their adventure, though this probably only takes a week or so. We are gone for a brief period one afternoon, the first day of the Millennial Fair. When we return, probably some hours later, Crono is arrested, and if we choose to serve our sentence until Lucca arrives to save him, he is jailed for three days. After he breaks out, he and the party travel here and there through the timeline. We spend at least one drunken—er, soup-bloated?—night in 65,000,000 BC, and another in Frog's burrow after giving him the repaired Masamune. Later, after a rough battle with Magus, we wake up once again in prehistory. After Crono dies, we awaken in the

Last Village of 12,000 BC. Finally, when we complete the sidequest to save Fiona's forest, we spend one fateful night in the woods, where Lucca gets her chance for a do-over. We end the game on the last night of the Millennial Fair for the Moonlight Parade. This gives us a bare minimum of six to eight days to complete our adventure. Damn, we can really hoof it! I did ignore those frequent visits to the inn—a player who likes clean sheets might return his party home months older than when they started. And if we task Robo with reforesting the land, he will have aged an extra 400 years.

Now, let's complicate this further.

The gates we travel through—and eventually the chronometer embedded in the Epoch—become fixed not to unchanging points in time, but rather to a specific active timeline. When we first return through the gate from 600 AD back to 1000 AD, for example, we don't return at the exact point we had left. Enough time has passed to alert the royal guards that something odd had happened to Marle, and Crono is arrested almost immediately. And the next time we use that gate from 600 AD to 1000 AD, the events of that farce of a trial have not been forgotten. All of the actions we take in each era remain constantly in effect. Without this fluidity, there would be no adventure at all—just a series of constantly unraveling plans, an endless and unplayable video game version of *Groundhog Day*.

So what does all this mean? It means that while our party members can change the world(s) around them for the better, the residents of those eras who reap the benefits *will never realize it*. And the ultimate irony of *Chrono Trigger*'s time-based altruism? *We are powerless to change our own pasts.* And even if we could, would we—like all of those time-muggles—forget that we had ever made those changes? We would forever be dissatisfied with our lots in life, never knowing how much our stations had improved.

THE FATED HOUR

YOU CAN'T TAKE IT WITH YOU. A maxim of transience and impermanence, of both pro- and anti-materialism at once. While funerary cultures across the globe still bury their dead with their treasured possessions, I remain unconvinced of the transferability of worldly goods into the afterlife—if there even is one.

At first glance, the afterlife of *Chrono Trigger* the game seems to have been rich. A few reincarnations for various game platforms have promised new added value to players while carrying over the best of their past lives. Chrono Trigger the *franchise* has given birth to new stories, for better or worse. For some players, official sequel *Chrono Cross* was a worthy continuation of the Chrono name, but to me it felt more like a clumsy tie-in that invalidated everything triumphant about *Chrono Trigger*. And there is still worse. The serial manga *Jikū Bōken Nuumamonjā*—perhaps localizable as *Space-Time Adventure Nu and Kilwala*—features the tiresome antics of two of the most familiar monsters in *Chrono Trigger*.

This comic was later adapted into an abysmal featurette known in some circles as the "*Chrono Trigger* anime," despite not featuring in any significant way the cast we've grown to love. I am tempted to blame *Nuumamonjā* for the death of the Chrono series, but it's more likely that lightning struck the Dream Team only once.

Fans seem to have treated the legacy of *Chrono Trigger* with more respect than its copyright-holders have. The sheer volume of unofficial art, fiction, music, comics, wikis, games, and criticism (like this book) attests to the influence that this game has had on the people who have played it. For the time being, *Chrono Trigger* has achieved a kind of temporary immortality through its fandom.

The karmic fate of Crono and company, luckily, is less complex than the game they star in. Each time we complete a full turn of the adventure, we have a chance to start over again. Not just from scratch, but rather with a "New Game +."

Crono still wakes up the same old way. "Good morning, Crono!" Our always unflappable mom is unfazed by all the items we seem to have acquired overnight. Her suddenly ultra-buff, filthy-rich, weapon-hoarding, women's-clothing-collecting son is the same as he was yesterday. *Does she even see?*

Our first New Game + slightly lifts the veil between worlds for Crono and those who join his party. A gate has appeared on Lucca's telepod, one that leads straight to Lavos. But Lucca displays no awareness of the anomaly, and neither does Marle until she joins Crono officially. There is a world behind this world, surely something unknown and exciting. If Crono and Marle travel through this new gate and can vanquish Lavos as a duo, then they'll reach what must be the closest thing *Chrono Trigger* has to a heaven. And yes, they can take all their items with them.

•

The in-game headquarters of the Dream Team is a repurposed End of Time, now populated by *Chrono Trigger* staff in the guise of mostly familiar sprites. Some of these creator demigods joke around with us, revealing their roles in our adventure, while others stump us with non-sequiturs. Still others are relieved that the game is over. "I've lost 22 pounds because of this game," laments field programmer Kazumi Kobayashi in the form of a fallen soldier, "You'd better be enjoying it!" Others complain about their graying hair, or just feeling *so fucking tired*. There's something amiss about the afterlife, and it feels hollow. This end-of-game End of Time is just an antechamber, however. Once we talk to all of its restless spirits, the tabernacle of creation is unlocked for us. We're about to meet our makers.

There they are, the three members of the Dream Team, here as an expanded pentad. The two newcomers are producer Kazuhiko Aoki—dressed in a partial tanuki suit emblazoned with a Chinese character,[16] and co-composer Nobuo Uematsu as semicorporeal Norstein Bekkler. But it is the three major creators of *Chrono Trigger* who should draw our attention. Here are the men who, traveling once upon a time to the United States to study the newest computer graphics, began enthusiastic discussions to make a game together. Drinking and chatting, these three gurus—Hironobu Sakaguchi, Yūji Horii, and Akira Toriyama—laid the broad foundations for what would, with the help of many minions, become *Chrono Trigger*. Flash forward several years from those first fateful sips of booze, and how do these men appear here, in this holiest of holies? As towering gods? As badass superbosses?

They are just men. Dumpy, un-*kawaii* caricatures of their real-world appearances. Surely, though, this disappointing trinity has something meaningful to say.

"Boy, it used to be that I'd get thinner after each game," whines Sakaguchi, "Now I'm gaining weight instead. Ack! I must be getting old." This is not the type of reassurance we want to hear from God. Hiding his face with a surgical mask, Toriyama gives a generic shoutout to his children. Horii, a nonsense riddle fit for a modern day Lewis Carroll:

---

16 The character 中, pronounceable as *naka* or *chū*, chiefly bearing the meaning of "middle" or "center." I have not deduced the meaning of Aoki's sprite.

One of these things is not like the others…
A Stapler, Mothra, and the Olympics.
SO… which one is it?

I have formulated my own tentative answer to Horii's riddle,[17] but does his Zen koan hint at greater meaning behind the universe, or does it instead reveal the nonsensicality of existence?

We have met our creators, and they are all too human. Luckily, we don't have to hang around this dull purgatory for eternity. Once we've spoken to all five Dream Team members, we are hastily told that we've been accepted as a member of the Team as well. After a speedrun of the credits—"since you blew through the game so fast"—we are rocketed back to the limbo of the title screen. Where, if we want, we can start all over again.

•

Chrono Trigger is a static game. Once we discover all the secrets, experience all the endings, there's little else

---

17 "Mothra, because she's boring!" The riddle is the same in Japanese, and my nonsense answer relies on a Japanese linguistics pun. Both "stapler" (*hochikissu*, ホッチキス) and "Olympics" (*Orinpikku*, オリンピック) contain the consonant-doubling "ッ," which can be described as a *tsumaru oto* (つまる音), or "a stopping-up sound." "Mothra" (*Mosura*, モスラ) does not contain ッ, so it does *not* stop up (*tsumaranai*). More punnily, *tsumaranai* means "uninteresting."

to do before it becomes repetitive. Those of us who began with the SNES version might upgrade to the DS version, and complete all the new quests this parallel universe offers. But how many times can we play *Chrono Trigger* before we move on? There are more games than this, and countless more adventures that lie outside of chunky gray cartridges.

All of us look back on our lives with a mixture of regret, satisfaction, and nostalgia for our achievements and our failures. Would we reset our lives with a chance to end up at that title screen of birth? And if we could find it, how do we decide between the possibilities of a fresh start at level 1, or the baggage of a New Game +?

We don't have that difficult decision. We don't get a chance to restart the journeys we began. But it's never too late for us to start leveling up, even if it means more grinding than we want out of life. But time is not on our side—no, it's not. We can't travel back to key moments and correct the errors of history, the mistakes of our pasts. We can't see what the future will hold and plan against it. The fate of our world is always dependent on now, and even this ever-present now will someday run out of time.

•

There is beautiful melancholy to endings.

In the game's most optimistic conclusions, the party gathers one last time at the end of the Moonlight

Parade, standing before the time rift that brought them all together. It will soon send them their separate ways. The celebratory music of the parade slowly dies out. Then, a twinkly but somber music box tune fades in—"Epilogue, To My Dear Friends." Marle is our emcee here, saying goodbye to each party member as Crono hangs back in silence. I start to wonder if I'd missed something big here—the story of Marle growing up from impetuous girl to capable young woman. But there's no time to ruminate on this. Friends are leaving.

Ayla and Kino race home, more than eager to get to work on making the baby who will eventually become Marle's ancestor. Princess Marle kisses her Frog goodbye, giving him one last invitation to straightness—much to his shocked embarrassment. Magus follows next with silent resolve to find his sister, the only person who gives him meaning. Finally, Lucca bids farewell to Robo, who stumbles with oily tears in his eyes through the gate that will separate him from the only family he has left. Toward a future that may erase him completely. One by one, our friends from past and future alike are gone.

"Do you remember that talk we had?" Lucca asks Crono and Marle.

"You mean about whether our lives flash by before we die?" Marle responds.

Neither have time to find a satisfactory answer, because another adventure is already beginning. Maybe

Crono's mom follows those cats we forced her to care for through the gate, so of course we're going to rescue her on an emergency time machine ride! Racing through the eras, we see our friends—Robo too!—making new beginnings for themselves. Or maybe it's that Marle gets swept up into the sky on an unexpected balloon ride! Failing to pull her back to the ground, Crono ends up holding onto her, the lovers floating high above the fireworks. The wistful sadness of *it's all over* becomes the giddy joy of *it's all happening so fast*.

I want these to overlap. I want to be forever putting things to rest while starting things anew. I want my life to flash by while I'm still living it. I wonder, though, if any of us have the strength to feel like this all the time. If we don't need times of silent reflection after the tale has ended.

•

The history of *Chrono Trigger* is not a simple summation of the game's plot and design, or how well it sold. There are stories behind every person who contributed to the development of this game and its release, behind every player who experienced it, behind every exasperated mother who waited in line to buy her son the game he absolutely had to have. I can't tell you most of these stories—but I can tell you my own. There is so much out there and I wanted to tell you *all of it*. I've tried to make this book a Gate Key, but in doing so I have become a gatekeeper, opening some doors to you and obscuring others behind false walls. I do not apologize for this.

I'll always treasure *Chrono Trigger* as an integral part of my gaming inventory, a key item that kept me questing and opened up new roads to adventure. But like many key items, there are only so many times I can use it before it becomes a fond, undiscardable souvenir.

Like a certain amphibian in a place far away from us, we have the difficult job of putting our ghosts to rest while still keeping their spirits alive within us. We constantly look forward, while celebrating the never-ending finality of things. And when the end comes— our real end, no matter what kind of ending it is!—we face it with courage.

NOTES

The Strong, Silent Type

Petri Lankoski's remarks on game engagement can be found in his article "Player Character Engagement in Computer Games" (*Games and Culture* 6:4, July 2011). Joseph Campbell's monomyth appears in his book *The Hero with a Thousand Faces*. Information about the "unhappy ending" originally planned for *Chrono Trigger* comes from an interview with story planner Masato Katō in the Japanese *Chrono Trigger: Ultimania*. The English translation by Cal Hampton is hosted here at the fansite Chrono Compendium: http://bit.ly/1bsOCGa. The first printing of this book mistakenly attributed the plan for Crono to die to game supervisor Yūji Horii and not story planner Masato Katō. Patrick Holleman's notes on Chrono Trigger's design are in his 2012 book *Reverse Design: Chrono Trigger*, available for purchase at thegamedesignforum.com.

Straight? White? Male?

Tanner Higgin explores Tolkien's and Lewis's European mythbuilding in "Blackless Fantasy: The Disappearance of Race in Massively Multiplayer Online Role-Playing Games" (*Games and Culture* 4:1. January 2009). Iwabuchi Kōichi talks about *mukokuseki* in his 2002 book *Recentering Globalization: Popular Culture and Japanese Transnationalism*. Tetsu Misaki writes about Mr. Popo and *Dragon Ball Z* in his Japanese-language book *Doragon Bōru no Mangagaku*, published by Sairyūsha in 2011. Miki Tanikawa's discusses the "science girl" stereotype in a June 16, 2013 New York Times article "Japan's 'Science Women' Seek an Identity" (http://nyti.ms/1gAefSP). Evan Lauteria's remarks on sexual normativity and silent protagonists appear in his paper "Sexuality and Sexual Orientation in Console and Computer Games," originally presented at the game studies conference "Videogames and the Alien/Other" in 2006. James Valentine talks about *okama* in "Pots and Pans: Identification of Queer Japanese in Terms of Discrimination" in the 1997 compilation *Queerly Phrased: Language, Gender and Sexuality*.

Steel and Pure Logic

Eric Yosomono's description of arrests in Japanese can be found on his blog Gaijinass in a January 2, 2011 post titled "7 Brutal Realities Regarding Arrest in Japan" (http://bit.ly/1czEoOR). Michael Fisch describes Christian style weddings in Japan in "The Rise of the Chapel Wedding in Japan: Simulation and Performance" (*Japanese Journal of Religious Studies* 28:1-2, 2001).

The Day of Lavos

The NHK's *Unforgettable Fire: Pictures Drawn by Atomic Bomb Survivors* was published by Wildwood House in 1981. It is the English translation of a Japanese book called *Gōka o Mita : Shimin no Te de Genbaku no E*, published in 1975.

Neuga, Ziena, Zieber, Zom

Christopher Steiner's "border zone" of localization appears in the chapter "Rights of Passage: On the Liminal Identity of Art in the Border Zone" in the 2001 book *The Empire of Things: Regimes of Value and Material Culture*. Ted (Thomas Edward) Woolsey's 1991 master's thesis at the University of Washington is called *The Rumbling of Modernism: Writers and the Great Kantô Earthquake of 1923*. I interviewed both Woolsey and Tom Slattery via email in late 2013.

Life by the Book

Here's a chronological list of the *Chrono Trigger* strategy guides (both Japanese and English) that I was able to consult:

- *Kurono Torigā Kōryaku Daitokushū* (Shūeisha, April 15, 1995) [*V-Jump* special issue]
- *Chrono Trigger: Super Famicom* (Shūeisha, April 25, 1995)
- *Chrono Trigger: The Perfect* (Shūeisha, June 1995)

- *Chrono Trigger Instruction Booklet* (Squaresoft, August 1995) [issued with cartridge]
- *Chrono Trigger Player's Guide* (Nintendo of America, October 1995)
- *Chrono Trigger: The Complete* (Shūeisha, 1999)
- *Final Fantasy Chronicles Official Strategy Guide: Chrono Trigger and Final Fantasy IV* (BradyGames, 2001)
- *Chrono Trigger: Perfect Bible* (Shūeisha, 2008)
- *Chrono Trigger: Ultimania* (Square Enix, 2009)

The End of Time

Yūji Horii revealed his basic premise of time travel in *Chrono Trigger* in an interview with Play Online, currently archived at the Internet Archive (http://bit.ly/1g2nomC). Masato Katō reminisced on development difficulties in a November 1999 interview with *Chrono Trigger* composer Yasunori Mitsuda. The Japanese version can be found on Mitsuda's homepage Our Millennial Fair (http://bit.ly/1bPYyUs); the English version is archived at the Internet Archive (http://bit.ly/1Xogfmt);

The Fated Hour

The collected nu/kilwala comics by Hiroshi Izawa and Akihiro Kikuchi were published as *Jikū Bōken Nuumamonjā* in 1998 by Shūeisha. The anime version was officially released in a compilation VHS *V Janpu V Fesu '96 Bideo*, also published by Shūeisha in 1996. Unofficial copies may be found on YouTube.

ACKNOWLEDGMENTS

First and foremost, many thanks to my family, and especially to my mom, Bet. Not just for always standing up for me, but also for standing in lines to buy me video games. To my husband Jayden Yamakaze, for becoming my permanent Player Two, and for always staying in co-op mode even when I throw down the controller in anger. To my friends who have supported me—particular shoutouts are owed to Brennan O'Rear, who introduced me to the evolving doctrine of cautious optimism, and to Aunim Hossain, a party member from a previous adventure who shared his love of RPGs with me. Deep gratitude to and admiration for both Ted Woolsey and Tom Slattery, for bringing *Chrono Trigger* to generations of North Americans and for their direct contributions to this book. To Gabe Durham for his constant editorial help and for taking a chance on me, and to Ken Baumann, for his encouragement and delightfully irreverent book design. To Maxwell McGee for his industry connections, and to Patrick Holleman for his game design expertise and enthusiastic input. To early readers James Davis, James Jacobo-Mandryk, Danielle McCormick, Ryan Plummer, and Wade Thiel, for their fact-checking and eagle-eyed copy editing. To Adam Robinson, for his pristine page design and last minute fixes, and to Christopher Moyer, for making this second printing look better than ever. There is not enough space to gives thanks to all those who deserve it, but if you're reading these words then you are among them.

SPECIAL THANKS

For making our first season of books possible, Boss Fight Books would like to thank Andrew Thivyanathan, Carolyn Kazemi, Cathy Durham, Ken Durham, Maxwell Neely-Cohen, Jack Brounstein, Andres Chirino, Adam J. Tarantino, Ronald Irwin, Rachel Mei, Raoul Fesquet, Gaelan D'costa, Nicolas-Loic Fortin, Tore Simonsen, Anthony McDonald, Ricky Steelman, Daniel Joseph Lisi, Ann Loyd, Warren G. Hanes, Ethan Storeng, Tristan Powell, and Joe Murray.

ALSO FROM BOSS FIGHT BOOKS